EFFEC
DECISION

Educated at St Paul's School, John Adair has enjoyed a varied and colourful career. He served in the Arab Legion, worked as a deckhand on an Arctic trawler and had a spell as an orderly in a hospital operating theatre. After Cambridge he became Senior Lecturer in Military History and Leadership Training Adviser at the Royal Military Academy, Sandhurst, before becoming Director of Studies at St George's House in Windsor Castle and then Associate Director of The Industrial Society.

In 1979 John became the world's first university Professor of Leadership Studies at the University of Surrey. He holds the degrees of Master of Arts from Cambridge University, Master of Letters from Oxford University and Doctor of Philosophy from London University, and he also is a Fellow of the Royal Historical Society.

In 2006 the People's Republic of China conferred on John the title of Honorary Professor of Leadership Studies in recognition of his 'outstanding research and contribution in the field of Leadership'. In 2009 the United Nations appointed him to be Chair of Strategic Leadership Studies at its central college in Turin.

www.johnadair.co.uk
www.adairleadershipdevelopment.com

EFFECTIVE DECISION MAKING

THE ESSENTIAL GUIDE TO THINKING FOR MANAGEMENT SUCCESS

JOHN ADAIR

PAN BOOKS

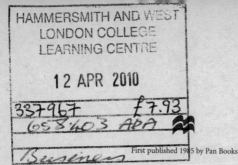
First published 1985 by Pan Books

This edition published 2009 by Pan Books
an imprint of Pan Macmillan Ltd
Pan Macmillan, 20 New Wharf Road, London N1 9RR
Basingstoke and Oxford
Associated companies throughout the world
www.panmacmillan.com

ISBN 978-0-330-50422-5

A CIP catalogue record for this book is available from
the British Library.

Typeset by Setsytems Ltd, Saffron Walden, Essex
Printed and bound in the UK by
CPI Mackays, Chatham ME5 8TD

CONTENTS

FOREWORD

Welcome to this fully revised edition of *Effective Decision Making*. It is a comprehensive guide to effective thinking in all its applied forms: making decisions, solving problems and generating new ideas. I hope you will enjoy reading it as much as I have enjoyed writing it.

At an early stage in my career I identified what I saw as the 'big three' subjects for training or development in what management theorist Douglas McGregor called the 'human side of enterprise', and over the years I haven't had cause to change my mind. They are Leadership, Decision Making and Communication. I later added a fourth – Time Management – because if you cannot manage your time correctly you cannot lead others, you will have no time to think and you will always be short of time to listen.

I see the 'big three' – or the 'big four' – not as separate subjects but as vital components of a single function: the general effectiveness that enables you to be a leader. In *Effective Leadership* I described the three overlapping functions at the core of leadership: achieving the Task, building the Team and developing the Individual, as depicted in the famous Three Circles model.

At first sight, decision making appears to be solely relevant to that first or top Task circle. But, as I shall be reminding you in this book, in the context of leadership decision making (which here includes problem solving and creative thinking) by necessity involves the Team and Individual circles as well. Remember, the circles are always interactive.

The message of this book is simple. With a little thought you can dramatically improve your powers as a decision maker. Of course, it can take years of practice, but if you apply the principles described here when working with your depth mind (see p. 98) or reflecting on your experience – successes as well as failures – you will make progress.

Who knows, you and I may one day acquire that attribute the ancient Greeks prized so highly in their leaders, which they called *phronesis*. We can best translate that Greek word as 'practical wisdom'. It is the product of a rare combination of keen intelligence, wide experience and profound goodness. On the following pages you will find pointers to lead you in this direction. It is a journey I am delighted to accompany you on.

John Adair 2009

INTRODUCTION

Decision making is an essential function of effective leadership. Together with communication it heads the list of abilities you should be seeking to develop as a successful leader. The aim of this book is to help you do just that.

The actual moment of decision cannot be studied – we are sometimes not even aware of it. Our primary concern here therefore must be the whole process by which minds are made up, the mental movements that lead to decisions: in a word, thinking.

For any leader, the kind of thinking that leads to action should be regarded as a demanding activity in its own right. 'If I have any advice to pass on it is this: if one wants to be successful one must think until it hurts.' So wrote Roy Thomson, one of the great businessmen of his day. 'Believe me', he added, 'this is hard work and, from my close observation, I can say that there are few people indeed who are prepared to perform this arduous and tiring work.'

Deciding implies a choice from several – or many – possibilities. Thinking is the preliminary work of weighing up the pros of cons for each course of action. A decisive person is someone who, when the time is ripe, has the power to stop thinking and start acting.

Decision making of this nature should not exhaust all of your thinking time. For one thing, it assumes that you know your objective: the mark you are trying to hit. Though that is not always the case. There is a perennial need in organizations to 'think until it hurts'about their purpose, aims and objectives.

Another important sphere for thinking that is not coupled to daily decisions concerns the generation of new ideas. Inventing new products, services and technologies, modifying or improving existing ones, seeing new opportunities and discovering fresh markets all require a capacity for original thought. Here, being overly preoccupied with decision making can actually be counter-productive.

On this sketch map we now need to place the sort of thinking appropriate to practical leadership that is commonly called problem solving. A problem literally means something thrown in front of you that requires attention, a solution or an answer. It is a very general word, as shown by the very varied ways we use it in everyday life: Jack's drinking problem, the problem of unemployment, the problem of motivating people, the problem of inflation, and so on.

Problems in these cases are loose descriptions of states of affairs that call for decision. Thus decision making and problem solving as activities tend to be conflated with each other; indeed, much established management literature seems to regard them as synonymous. I feel this is a mistake.

I'd like to suggest that as a business leader – I am using 'business' here in its widest sense of the field you are involved in – you are likely to be faced with two broad types of problem. The first is like an obstacle in your path. You have decided upon an objective and chosen a course of action: then, somewhere along the road you encounter an unforeseen block such as a strike in a supplier's factory or the unexpected illness of a key colleague. What should you do? Problems of this sort often derive from an earlier decision (the illness of your colleague might not have been a problem if you had not decided to, say, go on holiday for a week).

If you never decide anything you never have any problems. The mental processes for dealing with solving are the same as those used in decision making.

The second type of problem involves systems – something goes wrong with a mechanical system such as an assembly line or machinery. As a manager in this type of scenario, you are rather like a doctor dealing with the human body; you need to study the symptoms and diagnose the underlying cause(s) of the trouble. Only when these have been corrected will the health of the system be restored. Problem solving of this kind is heavily dependent on professional knowledge and case experience. As you rise higher as a leader in your field, however, it is an activity you are likely to delegate to specialists. Problem solving in systems situations, therefore, is not a major theme in this book

Many problems – crossword puzzles, for example – can be solved without having to take action. But decision implies action and change: life will not be quite the same again and it may very well be radically different. Thus, people who are very clever at solving academic-type problems may lack the qualities required to take decisions in situations involving uncertainty and risk.

The context of decision making for the manager is the subject of the first chapter of this book. In it I contrast the theory of the rational manager with some research into what managers actually do, mainly to get you thinking hard about how you use your time. I also underline the significance of decision making in this chapter.

The subsequent chapters review the basic functions of thinking – analysing, reasoning, synthesizing and thinking in wholes, imagining and valuing. These are described and illustrated with practical examples and case studies. For, where possible, I have drawn on the experience of those who have excelled in decision making or some other relevant form of thinking. Not all examples are taken from the world of work: you can stretch your mind more if you consider a wide range of analogies or models. To stimulate further thought I have included some exercises for you to tackle as you go through the book. You will, on occasion, also find Signposts, where you can take stock and decide which part of the book you would find it most useful to read next.

In Chapter 8 I explore the role of what I call the 'depth mind' in decision making, an aspect of thinking closely related to intuition that has received little attention. You can make progress in making more effective use of the unconscious mind if you are aware of its existence and understand how it works.

In the later chapters of the book, I focus upon decision making in the sense of choosing between feasible options; the nature of good reasoned argument about those courses of action; and how new ideas are produced. The final chapter is a summary, drawing together the threads and suggesting practical ways in which to maintain and improve your basic mental fitness. I hope you find it useful.

1

THE MANAGEMENT CONTEXT

'Without a leader, the birds do not fly far'
Chinese proverb

Thinking is not done in a vacuum. This book assumes a context: the manager at work.

Managers are subject to many pressures. They are interacting with their environment with particular ends in view. But that environment is subject to change, as are the ends of enterprise and the managers themselves. Therefore thinking for the manager is like handling a small ship in a rough sea, often without maps or charts. That is the test of true management.

In this chapter we look at the key factors that impinge upon – and often shape – the decision making aspect of the manager's job. Perhaps you will recognize yourself in this identikit picture. In the rest of the book we shall work on that picture until it becomes more to your liking.

What is management? All authors like to start with a definition. But in this case it might be more useful to look at what we know about managers, and the qualities they need to succeed.

THE CRUCIAL COMPETENCE

Everyone agrees that decision making and problem solving are among the core functions of the manager's job. By 'everyone' I mean the academics who have studied management and the people who manage. Let's concentrate on the latter.

One of the most sensible criterion we have for determining pay relativities is to go by the decision making content of jobs. A surgeon, an airline pilot and a refuse collector all take decisions. Why do we pay the first two more than the latter? Because their decisions involve life-and-death for us and because the knowledge required for their jobs takes many years to acquire. When a client complained to a famous painter about the fee he proposed to charge her for six hours of work on her portrait he replied, 'Not six hours, madam, but thirty years of experience.'

By the same token a builder responsible for a large town centre redevelopment project lasting three years will earn more than one who merely refurbishes kitchens. In life you will be paid according to the quality and quantity of the decisions you make within your sphere of work.

Decisions, therefore, are central to managing. One definition of management is 'deciding what to do and getting it done'. In any management situation a decision or series of decisions must precede implementation. The outcome in terms of success or failure, however, will depend on both the decision itself and your effectiveness in implementing it. That is where leadership or, influence, communication and motivation come into play. The first requirement for success in any enterprise, then, is high quality management decisions.

THE RATIONAL MANAGER

The decision maker, in the classic view of management, follows a logical or step-by-step sequence. He or she is completely rational with clear, unconflicting objectives and a perfect knowledge of the problem. All information is gathered and all possible solutions or courses considered.

In management theory the hallmark of the rational manager is that he or she makes a decision between choices in terms of their consequences or outcomes. When people talk about being rational in this context that is usually what they mean. If the objective is purely financial – to maximize profit – consequences can be assessed numerically and a simple choice made. If you can safely invest a large sum of money with a 10 per cent return in one stock or with 12 per cent in another, the choice is obvious – at least on purely rational grounds.

The rational manager in action

Imagine you are the owner of a small building firm. One day, you are told that the old lorry you have been using for the last eight years is on the point of falling to bits. You have a month at most to decide what to do. Here is a list of possible actions you can take. Which would you not do, and in what order would you work on the remaining items?:

1 Go and buy a new lorry from the nearest dealer.
2 Take a month's holiday in Spain.
3 Buy a farm instead.
4 Find out the cost of renting new vans of different types.
5 Work out what kind of lorry you need.

6 Ask the bank manager how much he will lend you.

7 Add up how much money you could afford to spend.

8 Find out the tax angles.

9 Get details of all possible types of suitable lorry, including price, fuel consumption etc.

10 Get three quotes for repairing your present lorry.

11 Take a cold bath.

12 Sell the business.

13 Carefully evaluate all your options.

14 Consult your staff.

15 Find out the cost of hay and a horse and cart.

The irrelevant items in the list are numbers 2, 3, 11 and 15. The information gained and the activity of tackling these items may be interesting and enjoyable but they are not vital to the decision. Whereas the remaining items are most certainly important.

The rational manager would start by defining the problem, in this case whether to buy a new lorry or repair the old one. They would then obtain all the relevant information (4, 6, 7, 8, 9) and draw up a list of all the reasonable alternatives available (13). Having evaluated the options they would make a decision and take some kind of action. This might be to sell the business or buy a new lorry from the nearest dealer or even to do nothing! The important point is that the decision is taken at the right time and is the best possible choice. What about consulting staff? That depends on the style of the owner; some always consult, some never do.

THE FIVE POINT PLAN

On Decision Making courses I have frequently asked managers to list the main stages they go through when making a decision or solving a problem. There is a general agreement that clusters around a Five Point Plan, as shown in the table below.

There is probably an element of unreality here in that the several thousands of managers who answered the question may have been telling me what ought to happen, rather than what actually does happen. They may have attended courses or read books on the subject, with both sources preaching the Five Point Plan.

Nevertheless, the very fact that there is a consensus on this sequence is significant. It means you can appeal to it in joint decision making or problem solving, and that it can serve as a frame of reference for a team working together. Moreover, it does reflect what many managers in many situations actually try to do.

FIVE POINT PLAN	
STEPS	**KEY ACTIONS**
Define objective	Specifying the aim or objective, having recognized the need for a decision.
Collect information	Collecting and organizing data; checking facts and opinions; identifying possible causes; establishing time constraints and other criteria.
Develop options	Listing possible courses of action; generating ideas.
Evaluate and decide	Listing the pros and cons; examining the consequences; measuring against criteria; trials; testing against objective; selecting the best.
Implement	Acting to carry out the decision; monitoring the decision; reviewing.

The Decision Making Model below shows a slightly expanded version of the Five Point Plan. ('Sense effects' here means having the awareness to pick up the signs or symptoms of an existing problem, long before the nature of the problem is clear.)

Using the Five Point Plan

If you happen to have attended a decision making meeting in the last week, try and recollect how far its chairman guided the group in the five phases. Alternatively, if you are involved in making a personal decision yourself, write it down, as far as you can, using the Five Point Plan as a framework.

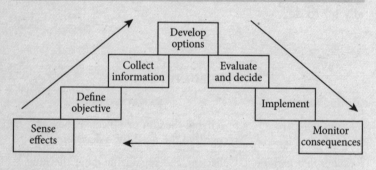

A decision making model

FACTORS THAT AFFECT DECISION MAKING

In decision making today, managers have to take into account a wider range of factors than was assumed in the early days of management science. An American researcher called Nicholas Nicholaidis analysed 332 administrative decisions taken by officials in the public sector. He found that, far from being based purely on logical grounds, decisions were informed by strong combinations of emotion, power politics, the influence of other people, and the individual decision makers' own values. Moreover, the decision makers rarely settled for the best or optimum solution as recommended by the management text-books, tending to look for a satisfactory compromise among two or more of the courses or solutions; namely, one(s) that:

- Agreed, at least to some extent, with their own personal interests, values and needs.
- Met the value standards of their supervisors.
- Were acceptable to both those who would be affected by the decision and those who had to carry it out.
- Looked reasonable in its context.
- Contained a built-in justification that would furnish an excuse, and possibly an avenue of retreat, in case the actual results of the decision turned out to be quite different from those anticipated.

How far Nicholaidis was an accurate and fair observer is open to debate, but this research is typical of much that emphasizes the apparently illogical elements at work in the manager's thinking, such as the presence of strong emotion and the influence of personal values.

There is one factor in particular that militates against a careful step-by-step approach to decision making – there is often not enough time. So you cannot gather all the important and relevant information, nor carry out a thorough evaluation of the choices. Managers agree that there often seems to be insufficient 'thinking time'.

The prominence of such phrases as 'influence of other people', and 'power politics' points to another missing key factor in the classic view of managerial decision making – the centrality of people. That is the theme of the next chapter. But it's worth noting here that taking the human factor into consideration does not necessarily imply that you are flying in the face of reason.

Rational thinking can also be contrasted with the kind of decision that seems to be taken without conscious reasoning, or *in spite of* the Five Point Plan rather than *through* it.

The essence of management, then, is decision making. In the classic view that process involves the Five Point Plan: Define objective, Collect information, Develop options, Evaluate and decide, and Implement. A rational approach to management emphasizes the importance of making the best choice by calculating the consequences. That is fine so long as you remember that the consequences that need to be considered are not solely financial: other benefits and losses must enter the picture. Moreover, many managers do not appear to reach decisions by a logical or step-by-step process, but, rather, rely more on flair and intuition. Indeed, there are pressures on managers, such as shortage of time, that can work against their following a systematic decision making process. These pressures can conspire to induce stress, which in turn can lead to poor quality thinking and indecisiveness. Time to think must be the priority for managers who want to become more effective, and therefore they must manage their time with that end in view.

PEOPLE ARE WHOLES, NOT SPARE PARTS

People can be difficult to manage. But they are also your enterprise's most valuable resource. All business involves co-operative effort. Management implies that you have people working under you, and probably beside you and above you. In the classic definition, management is achieving results through people.

Because other people are so central to a manager – in contrast to, say, an author, cartoonist, research scientist or university lecturer – they constitute another complete dimension to his or her thinking. The amount of time managers spend with people in meetings and interviews, unplanned discussions and on the telephone, is a simple recognition of that fact.

It is, however, important to remember that people are wholes, not parts. Organizations are groups of people out to achieve a limited purpose. As a manager you are asking people to contribute with part of themselves, not their whole selves. Therefore there may be a tension between their whole self and the limited part of the self you are taking on.

As a manager you are to some extent using other people as a means to an end, just as you yourself are being used by the shareholders or senior managers as a means to an end. But the first principle in any commonsense morality is that people should be treated as such, with all that this entails. Think of it as follows.

There are two sets of jagged rocks on either side of a comparatively narrow channel that you have to steer your ship through. On the one side is the old assumption that you are merely hiring 'hands' or 'time', chunks of some impersonal force called 'labour' or 'human resources'. On the other side is the assumption that you have bought the whole person, lock, stock and barrel, and that the interests of the individual are one and the same as those of the group.

This latter assumption may lead organizations to believe that they can and should mould people by a process of social engineering into 'company people' who will think, eat, sleep and dream company business. Here the business organization is forgetting that its relationship with the individual is basically contractual. To the individual concerned, it is not like belonging to a family, a church or a national community.

Of course, they may want to work beyond the call of duty, to the point where they can even be said to be exploiting themselves. But that is quite different from the organization *requiring* them to devote their whole life to its service and demanding the right to pry into their private life or their proper privacy as a person. People are under no obligation to have their opinions monitored or their mind explored.

A natural corollary to this is that the employee, whatever their rank or status, does not have the right to be their 'whole' self at work, regardless of the cost or inconvenience to others. The organization is not there to further self-fulfilment. It is there to achieve its proper purposes. In other words, the concept of a limited contract works both ways.

There is bound to be a *tension* between two ranges or families of values at work – the productivity values (money, goods and services) and the human values. But there need not be *a conflict* – in the sense of open war – between them. Balancing those values is central to the effective management of any organization.

Consider the views of a young trainee manager who graduated in English from Cambridge University.

Many graduates are compelled, indeed are glad, to accept the jobs in business which they are offered. But they remain unwilling to give up at a stroke the personal identities they have wrought through their education.

I would contend that graduates, while accepting jobs in business, do not immediately identify with the values of a business world. That is, they remain profoundly unconvinced of the efficacy of the profit motive as it applies to large corporations.

They retain their belief, albeit romantic, in the opportunity of the individual to express himself; and they remain suspicious of manipulative management techniques. In short, one might say that they feel more one of 'us', than part of 'them'.

Many graduates are now choosing a half-life; by day fulfilling the demands of the executive to the barest minimum, and retreating at nights and weekends to view quite objectively and dispassionately their career 'half'.

This is a quite new managerial schizophrenia that has mingled a private, radical disavowal of a business career with a public acceptance of market necessity, and its full ramifications have yet to be seen.

A senior manager, commenting on these remarks, said, 'Perhaps all students with these exceptions should remember that leaving university is only the end of the beginning. This bleating attitude will not earn much sympathy in the business world.' Would that view be closer to your own?

One way to banish this 'managerial schizophrenia' is to create as much overlap as possible between the 'wants' of the organization and those of the individual. It will then be natural for managers to apply all their brain power to their work. The individual will, in turn, strive to become a better decision maker, problem solver and creative thinker because he will, in an important sense, be working for himself as well as serving a common and worthwhile purpose. The sense of alienation, that great enemy of good work performance, will give place to a genuine and lasting job satisfaction.

INVOLVING WORK PEOPLE IN DECISIONS

Should this fuller involvement of the mind in one's work be confined to the manager?

At this point I would like to draw attention to the traditional distinction between managers and work people that used to prevail in old-fashioned manufacturing industries. Generally speaking, it went without saying that managers would feel involved and committed at work because they had to employ their minds to make decisions and solve problems. It was equally assumed that the 'workers', as they were known, would not feel so involved, because only their physical strength or manual dexterity was hired. They were hands not minds. Today, this old distinction between 'us' and 'them' has almost entirely disappeared.

In the last resort, whether you see people as your most important resource or not, depends on your belief in humanity. For my part I hold the belief that most people, irrespective of colour, creed or race, will respond to a leader's request for suggestions or ideas. For we are all born helpful. We only become unhelpful because of what parents or society do to us or because we have inherited a particularly unfortunate set of genes. But in general the human race is geared to help one another. That is why man is called a social animal. We could not have survived otherwise.

SUMMARY

Most organizations today are people businesses. If nothing else, people are one of their bigger costs. It is essential, therefore, for enterprises to create within themselves an environment or climate that really stimulates people to use their brains to the maximum. Leadership and good communications are necessary to create those conditions. Once these are in place, people will produce better corporate decisions, a higher standard of problem solving and increase creative thinking and innovation. Work will be more fun too.

KEY POINTS: THE MANAGEMENT CONTEXT

- Decision making is integral to leadership in all fields and all levels – team, operational (or middle management) and strategic. That doesn't mean that the leader or manager should make the decisions without consultation – far from it. But the leader is accountable for seeing that the necessary decisions are made and implemented.

- Simple frameworks can be very useful. The Five Point Plan is such a framework. It breaks down decision making into five elements: Define objective, Collect information, Develop options, Evaluate and decide, Implement.

- Although in real life the power of decision making can appear to be untidy it should still always exhibit those five elements – it should, in other words, have an underlying order. If one of the elements is omitted or poorly done, the whole process founders on the rocks.

- Decisions of any importance require a considerable amount of time in order to get them right. Time pressure can induce stress, which in turn lowers the quality of thinking in the decision making process. So good time management is essential.

- People are wholes not parts. They bring to work with them their intelligence, experience, goodwill, helpfulness and creativity. All leaders should be grateful of this rich human resource.

The task of leadership is not to put greatness into people but to elicit it, for the greatness is there already.

John Buchan

2

KNOW YOUR MIND

'Thought, I love thought . . .
Thought is the welling up of unknown
life into consciousness,
Thought is the testing of statements
in the touchstone of conscience,
Thought is gazing onto the face of life,
and reading what can be read,
Thought is pondering over experience,
and coming to conclusion.'

D.H. Lawrence

You can start to improve your decision making ability by sharpening the thinking tools that Nature and education have equipped you with. This chapter offers a sketch map of how your mind – and the minds of every colleague in your organization – actually works. We shall then consider the main components, so to speak, of the model. To become more effective as a thinker you will need to separate out and sharpen up major mental abilities that, in the actual processes of decision making or problem solving, are virtually indistinguishable.

Understanding how your mind works when it is thinking about a decision or problem is not easy; it is like trying to jump on your shadow. Most of us are not introspective by nature though you shouldn't let that prevent you from becoming more aware of the range and depth of your basic mental functions. The secret is not solitary introspection, which may merely tend to make you a bit more introverted, but to try to catch your mind off-guard when it is going about its business.

You can think of your mental functions as being rather like a football team before the camera. They are anxious to pose for you, arms folded and faces smiling, perhaps with a silver cup or two at their feet. But that kind of photography session tells you nothing about their footballing skills, nor, indeed, the game of football itself. You have to see them struggling against another team, passing the ball from one to another, giving ground and then surging forwards, obeying rules and breaking them, to come near to understanding what football – or, by analogy, the mind at work – is all about.

Try the following exercise. It brings some important mental functions into play.

EXERCISE 1: Who is going to Barker Street?
Five taxi-drivers have been summoned to pick up five fares at a London club. On arrival, they find that their passengers are slightly intoxicated. Each man has a different first and last name, a different profession, a different destination; and each man's wife has a different first name.

Unable to determine who's who and who's going where, the taxi-drivers ask you to find out: Who is the baker? What is Bert's last name? Who is going to Barker Street? You collect these facts from the passengers:

1 Brad is married to Betty.
2 Barbara's husband gets into the third taxi.
3 Bart is a banker.
4 The last taxi goes to Barton Street.
5 Beatrice lives in Burton Street.
6 The butcher gets into the fourth taxi.
7 Bob gets into the second taxi.
8 Bernice is married to the broker.
9 Mr Barker lives in Burton Street.
10 Mr Burger gets into the taxi in front of Brenda's husband.
11 Mr Bunger gets into the first taxi.
12 Mr Baker lives in Burbon Street.
13 The barber lives in Baker Street.
14 Mr Baker gets into the taxi in front of Mr Burke.
15 The barber is three taxis in front of Brian.
16 Mr Burger is in the taxi in front of the butcher.

If you have completed the exercise successfully in 20 minutes you have done well; 30 minutes is average, while 15 minutes or less is exceptionally good. Check your answers by turning to page 174. No cheating allowed!

BRAIN POWER

When working on the above exercise you were deploying a formidable amount of brain power. The brain contains around 10,000,000,000 neurons, or nerve cells. According to some scientists, we lose about 10,000 brain cells a day, but so great is our natural supply that, at 80 years of age, we will only have lost about 3 per cent of our brain capacity. If you sat down and counted each brain cell in your head, at the rate of one a second, you would still be counting in 30,000 years time.

Each neuron looks like a tiny starfish or octopus, with

synapses – places where the nerve cells join – lining its feelers. Each cell is capable of linking up with about 10,000 of its neighbours. That gives you an astronomical figure of possible combinations: 1 followed by 10 million kilometres of standard typewritten noughts. To put it another way, the number of possible connections in a single brain, is larger than the number of atoms presumed to exist in the entire universe. Chemical reactions involving somewhere between 100,000 and about one million cells were going on in your head at any given moment while you were tackling that problem of who goes to Barker Street.

The difference between brain and mind can be easily illustrated by thinking of a television set. If you open up the back – all those coloured wires and circuits – you are in the realm of brain research. The neurosurgeon is like the electrician who can repair the set. If you look at the screen of the television, however, you are in the realm of mind. It has the dimension of meaning. It is, of course, the workings of mind, rather than the brain as such, that is the central concern in this book.

What brain research suggests, however, is that our minds have almost limitless potential. Most of the problems we have in thinking are not because of any fundamental short-comings in this biological super computer of ours, but because we don't know how to use it effectively.

THREE FAMILIES OF ABILITIES

The mind has several different ways of working that can be called meta-functions or families of abilities. The exercise above obviously required you to use your analytical abilities as a thinker, and also to think logically, which is a near relation to analysing. So two members at least of the most prominent family of thinking ability – the analysers – were hard at work. But other abilities are also in use when you are thinking to some purpose. There are three family groups of ability in total, which are as follows:

Analysers

The prime ability of the analyser is to separate a whole into its component parts. Analysers are like ants. They can break down anything complex into its simple elements. The word itself comes from the old Greek verb meaning 'to loosen' or 'to break up'.

Synthesizers

The central ability of the synthesizer is the reverse of the analyser, namely to think and form wholes. In the synthesizing mind, components or parts are assembled together. The Greek verb that 'synthesize' is derived from means 'to piece together'. (This subject is dealt with more fully in Chapter 4, which I have preferred to call 'Holistic Thinking' because of my reservations about the term 'synthesizing' – see p. 51.)

Valuers

Valuers revolve around the perception of value, worth or significance. They include all forms of judging, criticizing and evaluating. Their 'relatives' do the actual measuring, counting and testing, work that the valuers often regard as beneath their dignity.

Each of these meta-functional groups is the subject of following chapters, so I shall not pause to illustrate them further now. But you may like to reflect further on them for a few moments and try to decide which of the three kinds of ability are your strongest and weakest.

USING YOUR DEPTH MIND

The depth mind is an unfamiliar phrase to most people. I have coined it to stand for those unconscious and subconscious parts of our minds that actually work for us. The term has been derived by analogy with the sea: the three families we have been looking at are abilities of the *conscious* mind that goes on the surface; the *subconscious* is the depth of a few fathoms where the light penetrates, while the *unconscious* is the deeper recesses into which we cannot see. Physiologically speaking, there is some evidence that depth mind thinking takes place within the inner part of the brain in both left and right hemispheres.

A vital function of the depth mind is memory. One of the mysteries of the mind is how we can recall things so swiftly on demand. If you are asked a fact, such as someone's name, you may often say (if you are like me), 'Give me a minute or two and I'll remember it.' A few minutes later the name pops into your conscious mind. Amazing.

Memory in its various forms as our private data bank plays a central part in our thinking, but is not the only contribution of the depth mind to effective mental activity. Following popular versions of Freud, who did more than anyone else to put the unconscious mind on the map, we tend to think of the unconscious as a kind of dustbin for our early personal frustrations. Into it drops all our mental rubbish – the bruised egos, the damaged wishes, the broken loves, the resentments, fears, hatreds and rages of our childhood. We then force down the lid on these suppressed feelings. But they erupt again in our dreams and in various forms of behaviour, such as the celebrated 'Freudian slips'. We have to remember, however, that Freud based his conclusions on his study of mentally ill patients.

To counter this rather negative image of the unconscious, later Freudian psychologists felt it necessary to coin yet another word – the *preconscious*. This stands for the realm where helpful subliminal thinking takes place, and is roughly equivalent to my own term, the depth mind.

The most interesting manifestation of this more helpful depth mind work is what we often call creative thinking. No one knows quite how the depth mind goes about its work. We do know, however, that it is capable of synthesizing apparently unrelated pieces into quite complicated jigsaw puzzles of meaning.

Robert Louis Stevenson described his own methods in imaginative work in this way. 'Unconscious thought, there is the only method: macerate your subject, let it boil slow, then take the lid off and look in – and there your stuff is, good or bad.'

The depth mind can both supply you with the seed of an idea and carry out an often intricate process of synthesis for you over a period of time. Both contributions are present in this passage by Lewis Carroll:

I was walking on a hillside, alone, one bright summer day, when suddenly there came into my head one line of verse – one solitary line – 'For the Snark was a Boojum, you see'. I knew not what it meant, then: I know not what it means, now: but I wrote it down: and, some time afterwards, the rest of the stanza occurred to me, that being its last line: and so by degrees, at moments during the next year or two, the rest of the poem pieced itself together . . .

I suggest that the depth mind can also analyse and value. In the former respect it can be compared to your stomach, which is fed with powerful enzymes that can break down the meals it is given. The analogy of digestion, the process of making food absorbable by dissolving it and breaking it down into simpler chemical compounds, seems especially apt.

With regard to valuing it is again impossible to be precise about what goes on. What is clear, however, is that our values inhabit our deeper minds and are often obscure to us until we do something or have to choose between two alternatives. Rationally we may believe (quite rightly) that decisions should be made on the basis of our values. It is often the case, however, that the decision comes first and then it tells us something about what our values really are. There is another related phenomenon here, namely that the act of decision in itself somehow confers value – 'Because I have chosen Smith as branch manager therefore he must be good.'

Using your depth mind in sleep

You may have had the experience of 'sleeping on' some decision or problem and finding that your mind has made up itself next morning. If you haven't, give it a try. The depth mind principle can also be used to memorize material. Just before you go to sleep, read what you have to learn, preferably out loud, and as you settle down concentrate on the material. As soon as you wake try to recall what you read – you may be surprised at how much you have remembered.

Can we develop this immense reserve power of our depth minds? Yes, within reason. Some people are more gifted in that way than others. But awareness of the part played by the subconscious, coupled with friendly interest in how it works, can set you on the path to self-development. You will find more specific suggestions later in the book.

MANAGING EMOTION

Thinking and emotion or feeling are often contrasted. But the mind is one. It is not surprising, therefore, that there is a complex relationship between thinking and emotion. It is important for anyone who wishes to improve their thinking to understand this relationship.

Emotion, along with motive, concerns things that move you. Emotion is the partly mental, partly physical response of being stirred up by someone or something. Physical danger or threat, as we know, produces a stirring up of emotion: strong feelings of fear and physiological changes that prepare your body for immediate vigorous action. If prolonged, such experiences may add up to stress.

Emotion carries a stronger implication of excitement or agitation than feeling, which suggests that our most powerful emotions lie dormant in the depths of our minds and are only stirred up on rare occasions. It may be helpful to think of the two in terms of the weather. Emotions are rather like strong winds, raging thunderstorms or blazing heat, while feelings are breezes, showers and the warmth of sun on the skin.

As we know, feelings and emotions accompany thinking. An apparently simple problem that resists repeated attempts at being solved will induce feelings of frustration. Thinking can be painful and it can be pleasurable. Indeed, it can be so pleasurable that it becomes addictive. There are people who are completely hooked on the hedonistic pleasures of thinking. As decision means an end to thinking and the beginning of action, they tend to resist that evil hour by always finding an excuse for more talk! At the other extreme are the people who find that thinking hurts, in the sense of giving them a physical headache or being just unpleasant. Therefore they avoid it!

There is one practical point about emotions. Highly creative people report something that has been called the hedonic response. This is the feeling of being on the right track – an advance payment, if you like, of the emotional rewards of success. Sometimes, then, our emotions refuse to adopt the role of 'full supporting cast'. They become pioneers or scouts reporting back to us that we are making progress even though the rational faculties of the mind are still in the dark.

ROADBLOCKS TO LEARNING

One aspect of emotion touches on your success or failure in studying this book, so I must deal with it now – the fear of the difficult. As such it is one of the hydra-heads of that monster 'Fear' that slumbers in the capacious caves of our unconscious minds. In his inaugural address on 4 March 1933, as the world slid further into Depression, President Roosevelt told the American nation in ringing tones: 'Let me assert my firm belief that the only thing we have to fear is fear itself.' There is no better motto for a thinker.

Take languages. 'Learning French is too difficult for my poor brain', an export manager once said to me. He was wrong. His brain could do it – he could not. The capacity of the brain in this regard is almost limitless. One Victorian linguist was able to speak 200 languages. It is theoretically, possible to know a vocabulary of about 800,000 words in English, but most of us operate with far fewer than 20,000.

Such remarkable feats pose some key questions. If brains such as this differ only slightly from our own, what spare capacity for learning does the average person waste? And why? Either he or she is afraid of the mental effort involved, or possibly they have tried it before and been unsuccessful – through not trying hard enough or indeed because of the wrong kind of instruction. They may have been taught by a poor teacher whom they loathed.

SUMMARY

You should now have a clearer understanding of how the human mind works when it is thinking to some purpose. You should have identified the principal skills that have to be developed and may also have begun to form some picture of your personal mental profile. Where do your strengths and weaknesses as a thinker lie?

This chapter should also have changed your attitude to those who work with you or under you. Everyone else in the workforce has 10,000,000,000 brain cells like you. Employing such formidable minds probably constitutes your organization's highest cost. What are the implications of this for both you as a manager and your organization? Surely that you should do all in your power to harness the brain power of every team member to the task in hand.

KEY POINTS: KNOW YOUR MIND

• Research using MRI scanners continues to map the brain areas associated with certain mental functions. But we also have some knowledge of the mind as opposed to the brain. The relationship between brain and mind remains mostly a mystery. Our concern in this book is with the work.

- When your mind is thinking to some purpose there are three meta-functions or families of mental skills at play: analysing, synthesizing and valuing.
- *Analysing* is essentially separating, dissecting or taking things apart to see what they are made of. *Synthesizing* is essentially putting things together, assembling, joining up. *Valuing* is essentially assessing the worth of something according to some scale of reference.
- When we think we are constantly switching from one 'musical key' of thinking to another, though we are seldom aware of doing so.
- The human mind can think purposively on different levels of consciousness. Quite a lot of analysing, synthesizing and valuing is done at a subliminal or less than conscious level. I call this the Depth Mind. It is especially associated with memory, intuition and creativity.
- Emotion or feeling can encourage and fuel effective thinking but negative emotions – fear in all its forms – have mostly bad effects. As a leader you need to be in complete command of yourself to ensure that negativity doesn't take over.
- Knowledge of the range, depth and capability of your own mind gives you knowledge of all other human minds – not least those of your colleagues at work.

Thought is not a trick, or an exercise, or a set of dodges
Thought is a man in his wholeness wholly attending.

D. H. Lawrence

3

ANALYSING

'I keep six honest serving-men
They taught me all I knew;
Their names are What and Why and When
And How and Where and Who.'
Rudyard Kipling

For anyone who means business having a good analytical mind is essential. This chapter further describes the purpose or role of analysis in thinking. When you have finished it you should have a fuller understanding of analytical ability and a working idea of how good you are at it. Competent analysing is especially important to all managers because it leads to clarity of thought.

What it Takes for Top Jobs, opposite, shows 25 attributes listed by 120 executive heads of Britain's largest private and public industrial organizations in order of value for their own work. Now put two marks on a scale of 0 to 10 beside them expressing the degree to which you think they can be developed by practical and professional experience as opposed to academic work and examinations. For example, if you think astuteness is overwhelmingly developed by academic work you may give it a mark of 9 out of 10 in the 'academic 'box and 0 out of 10 in the 'professional experience' box.

CHECKLIST:
What it takes for top jobs

Ranking of most valuable attributes at the top level of management	Attribute developed mainly by academic work	Attribute developed mainly by professional experience
1 Ability to take decisions	☐	☐
2 Leadership	☐	☐
3 Integrity	☐	☐
4 Enthusiasm	☐	☐
5 Imagination	☐	☐
6 Willingness to work hard	☐	☐
7 Analytical ability	☐	☐
8 Understanding of others	☐	☐
9 Ability to spot opportunities	☐	☐
10 Ability to meet unpleasant situations	☐	☐
11 Ability to adapt quickly to change	☐	☐
12 Willingness to take risks	☐	☐
13 Enterprise	☐	☐
14 Capacity to speak lucidly	☐	☐
15 Astuteness	☐	☐
16 Ability to administer efficiently	☐	☐
17 Open-mindedness	☐	☐
18 Ability to 'stick it'	☐	☐
19 Willingness to work long hours	☐	☐
20 Ambition	☐	☐
21 Single-mindedness	☐	☐
22 Capacity for lucid writing	☐	☐
23 Curiosity	☐	☐
24 Skill with numbers	☐	☐
25 Capacity for abstract thought	☐	☐

Check your answers against those of the chief executives (p. 176) and you will see that analytical ability is high on the list of most valuable attributes at number 7. But the chief executives believed that professional experience alone played only a small part in developing it. Do you agree with that conclusion?

Incidentally, the chief executives in the survey placed weight on passing examinations at school, college or university, but more as a test of character than of intelligence. In the case of professional qualifications these were valued as giving precise information about whether or not a person has the particular knowledge needed for a particular job. It fell to a member of a control group of sixty-six novelists and poets, John Wain, to give the most eloquent defence of examinations as tests of personality and character: 'To be successful in examinations of any kind means self-discipline, capacity to do unpalatable work, ability to concentrate and willingness to think about something other than yourself – all useful in any kind of situation and for any kind of person.' Academic work does shape, and examinations do test or reveal, our natural ability to think analytically.

IDENTIFYING THE HALLMARKS OF A GOOD ANALYTICAL MIND

How do you spot a good analytical mind in a team member or in someone applying for a job? First, we have to define what we mean by analytical ability.

Many people think of analysis as simply taking things to bits, like a child dismantling a toy. But it is much more than that – when analysing you are looking for something. What your quarry actually is will depend on the nature of the case, but you may be:

- Establishing the *relationship* of the parts to each other and to the whole.
- Finding the true *cause* or causes of the problem.
- Identifying the *issue* at stake, the 'either – or'upon which a decision must rest (what a good trial judge does).
- Discovering a *law* in nature.
- Searching for the *principles* behind experience.

These general points can be illustrated by examples drawn from particular fields, as shown in The Uses of Analytical Thought in Different Fields, over the page.

The achievements of analytical thought in scientific research are often spectacular. Incidentally, you may find it encouraging to reflect that success in examinations, like early precocity, is an unreliable guide to intellectual ability: a survey of Fellows of the Royal Society has shown that many of them possess only mediocre degrees.

Take one achievement in the field of biochemistry – the chemistry of life. The building blocks of virtually all life – from bacteria to humans – are cells. The nature and tasks of each cell are determined by its genes. The genes are long chains of the chemical called DNA, the famous 'double helix'. Each chain has only four types of 'link' (in fact, four chemical groups), but the links can be strung together in an almost infinite number of different sequences. The instructions that tell each cell how to reproduce itself lie in the exact sequence of those links. This formula charts the sequence of links in one of the simplest forms of life – a virus only one-millionth of an inch across. As a computer printout, this formula is 15 metres long. A comparable printout for the genes bearing the instructions to make a human being would stretch 10,000 miles, or almost halfway round the earth. It is for working out a way of charting these sequences – the code of life – that Dr Frederick Sanger

THE USES OF ANALYTICAL THOUGHT IN DIFFERENT FIELDS	
FIELDS	**ACTIVITY**
Chemistry	The resolution of a chemical compound into its elements and any foreign substances it may contain.
Optics	The resolution of light into its prismatic constituents.
Literature	The critical examination of any production, so as to exhibit its elements in simple form.
Grammar	Determining the elements composing a sentence or part of it.
Mathematics	The resolving of problems by reducing them to equations.
Philosophy	Resolving complex expressions into simpler or more basic ones.

of the Medical Research Council was awarded his second Nobel Prize.

Ten thousand million viruses could occupy the space within this asterisk ✱, each with a gene chain that would take four pages of computer printout to chart it. Sanger analysed just one virus, Phi-X-174, into its 5,386 sub-units. Over the years he improved his analytical techniques dramatically. At the beginning it took him a year to chart 50 sub-units of such a virus. Today up to 1,000 sub-units can be mapped in a day.

Sanger attempted to map the sequence of the twenty amino acids that are sub-units of the protein insulin. It turned out to be a fortunate choice: as proteins go, insulin is a comparatively small molecule. Even so, sequencing a protein was so formidable an undertaking that no more than a couple of points in a chain had ever been determined before.

Sanger had to develop chemical analysis techniques from scratch; and even identifying the easiest links – the amino acids at the ends of the chain – took months. It took him ten years to work out the complete structure.

To carry through, almost single-handedly, a research project of this length, with all its inevitable frustrations and setbacks, requires staying power of a high order. It is a quality Sanger possessed in abundance. 'I am', he said, 'very strongly self-motivated.'

Sanger's story shows us that analytical ability by itself, together with the capacity to develop and employ advanced analytical techniques, is not enough for real achievement as a thinker: you need flair or luck, perseverance and considerable self-motivation as well.

ANALYTICAL ABILITY IN BUSINESS LEADERSHIP

Analysing plays a central part in problem solving. The sifting process of separating facts from opinions or suppositions, pulling the elements of the problem apart, are happening as you work your way towards the heart of the problem. Your mind has to work like a shoal of piranha fish, stripping the problem down to its essentials.

A less common form of analysis, seen only in an exceptional thinker, is the ability to think for yourself as if from first principles. The hallmarks of a mind of this kind are simplicity, originality, coupled with great clarity. As one such thinker once told me, 'I have to spend a lot of time making things clear to myself. I go back to basic principles, but then they are so obvious that no one is interested.'

Consulting is a profession that calls for a high order of analytical skills, whether the consultant is in medicine, technology or business. There was once a company that sold iron bedsteads all over Britain. In spite of many actions, sales were falling. So a management consultant was hired to identify the cause. He knew about analysis and fact gathering so he collected detailed statistics relating to the sales force – number of salesmen, number of customers, miles travelled, calls made, commission earned and so forth. He concluded that the salespeople in Scotland and Wales were less effective than those in England and recommended they be replaced. But it soon became obvious that the new salesmen fared no better than their predecessors. The problem had nothing to do with the quality of the sales force. The root cause of the company's difficulty lay in the market place: iron bedsteads were going out of fashion.

The consultant above was rather like a medical counterpart trying to cure a painful foot by amputating it. It solves the apparent problem, but it's a rather drastic action for a badly fitting shoe.

Apart from analysing problems when they occur, do you set aside time to analyse what is going on in your own field to determine the underlying simple principles? Too much of this kind of activity probably leads to neglect of normal workload, but now and again it is very helpful.

You may question why a person who thinks as if from first principles should be deemed original. But our education does not train us to do that. We are lumbered with a mass of secondary or derived knowledge, most of which will soon be out-of-date. Our desire to confirm socially and mentally with each other also militates against such clear thinking. We are not taught to think for ourselves. You may recall the horrified reaction of the famous poet Shelley's mother when discussing her boy's future education:

Friend: 'Oh, send him somewhere where they will teach him to think for himself.'

Mrs Shelley: 'Teach him to think for himself? Oh, my God, teach him rather to think like other people.'

LEARNING TO ASK YOURSELF QUESTIONS

Thinking involves asking questions and trying to find answers to these questions. By 'asking questions' I don't necessarily mean using interrogative sentences. A genuine question demands an answer. To be thinking hard about something is to be in a questioning frame of mind. In order to get into that state you need to be puzzled about something. It could be how to start the car engine, or how to make a million dollars by a certain date, or how best to learn Japanese. You might be puzzled about who to promote, or why globules of air gather in sheet glass when it is being manufactured in a certain way.

The original question should then lead to a host of analytical questions, the piranha fish of the mind. These will be addressed to ourselves and to other people in an attempt to strip the matter down to the bare bones. Textbooks on decision making and problem solving usually supply long checklists of such questions but you shouldn't find them necessary if you have grasped the principle of articulating questions. It sometimes helps to say them aloud and listen to your own questions, or to write them down.

In the early days you can borrow questions from other

people, such as 'When did the problem first arise?' But, with practice, you should be able to develop your own portfolio of analytical questions to bring to any problem or situation. They are your mental tools or spanners. Some of them, you will find, fit a much wider range of situation than others. Go back to those magic words: Who? Which? Why? (and Why not?) When? Where? And How?

Analysing is such a basic part of our mental equipment that we tend to take it for granted. We forget that it can become limited in range and blunted at the edge. Aim to take a greater pride in your analytical ability and develop it whenever you get the chance.

THE ANALYTICAL METHODS OF LOGICIANS

The logician is especially concerned with what can be properly concluded from statements or propositions. In formal logic a set of two or more propositions and a conclusion is called a *syllogism*. Here is an example:

> All coins are round (major premise)
> You have a coin in your pocket (minor premise)
> Your coin is round (conclusion)

The relationship between the premises and the conclusion, or what they entail, is often called the inference.

The fact that academic logicians use these rather trivial-looking examples and that they tend to emphasize the formal relationship between statements should not blind us to the fact that they are struggling with a central theme in all our quests for truth, namely the *relation of the general to the particular*. In the real world we sometimes think in syllogisms without being aware of it.

One result of disciplining your mind to logical thin. a greater awareness of the part that premises play, especi. the kind that are generalizations. You will have noticed that the major premise above is false: all coins are not round. Therefore the argument based upon it collapses like a pack of cards.

The danger of holding a large stock of unsubstantiated generalizations in your mind is that you might start using them as premises. 'No, Miss Jones, I cannot offer you a manager's job in the finance department. For one thing, women just can't count, they aren't really numerate, you know. Also, I would have to send you on an expensive course, and all women leave to have babies just when they are fully trained. I expect you'll report me to the Equal Opportunities Commission – all malicious women do – but I promise you that they will not find me prejudiced. I pride myself on having an open mind.'

What goes wrong in reasoning or argument, then, can usually be traced to unsound premises or faulty logical steps. More often than not the reasoning is sound, it is the premises that must be examined.

Before moving on from formal logic there are two further lessons to be learnt by the manager. The first stems from a study of how logicians go about analysing arguments (see Filleting arguments, below) and the second is a useful summary of two directions in thinking, called inductive and deductive reasoning.

FILLETING ARGUMENTS

A good fishmonger can fillet a fish for you in a few seconds so that you see the hard, bony skeleton. It is a useful skill for a thinker. Logicians do it by reducing arguments to a gebra. It is then much easier to detect any

outstanding manager he would be
o the board.
He has been made a director.
Therefore, Jones is an outstanding manager.

This fallacious mode of argument is soon revealed by its skeleton:

If A, then B.
B.
Therefore A.

Of course, it is quite possible that Jones *is* an outstanding manager, but that conclusion is not a necessary inference from the reasoning offered. If we know it, we know it on other grounds.

Logical reasoning, then, centres upon what may or may not be properly concluded or inferred. It can be called 'consecutive thinking' because it is concerned with thinking in steps, the last step not being immediately apparent when you first embark on the journey. Algebra or mathematics method is therefore essentially logical, with letters or numbers in place of words as its elements.

Two other terms from the realm of logic are worth knowing: deductive and inductive reasoning, or deduction and induction. They are both ways of inferring things. Deduction means drawing a particular inference from a general proposition, while induction is the opposite: forming a generalization by considering a number of particular instances. The latter used to be regarded as the core of scientific method. Research activities – whatever the kind

– provide good ex-amples of induction. It would be an instance of deduction, for example, if we said: 'All salesmen like fast cars. Fred does not like fast cars and therefore he is no salesman'. The conclusion is, of course, invalid in this case. A correct deduction is present in the following syllogism: 'All ordinary shareholders are entitled to vote at the annual general meeting. All the directors are ordinary shareholders. Therefore, all directors are entitled to vote at the annual general meeting.'

Lewis Carroll produced some wonderful examples of arguments in deductive logic, including this: 'No one takes in *The Times* unless he is well educated. No hedgehogs can read. Those who cannot read are not well educated. Therefore, no hedgehog takes in *The Times*.'

In contrast to this kind of thinking, inductive logic at work can be seen in areas such as test marketing where a new or modified product is sold in a very small part of a company's market to see if it has any 'customer appeal'. The reasoning here follows this line: 'The new product sells very well in the North-east and the South-west. There is no reason why it should not sell well nationally'.

Other examples of fields where this kind of reasoning is used include product development, opinion surveys, market research and all the work that goes on in all the laboratories around the world. The aim is to make a prediction about the behaviour of everything or everybody in a particular class, by studying a small sample of that class.

In summary, logical thinking in the sense of being able to draw proper conclusions from information or evidence (as contrasted to general or particular premises of a lecture room nature), is central to most professions, from car mechanics to police detectives. That ability is vital to managers as well. Do you have it?

EXERCISES 2–6: How good is your logical thinking?
You have already had one attempt at logical thinking (on p. 15). Armed with that experience and the knowledge in this chapter – together with a piece of paper and pencil – you shouldn't have too much difficulty with the following exercises. The answers are on p. 177 and the time allowed for them together is 10-15 minutes as long as you have not seen any of the problems before.

2. Each of three friends – Mr Carpenter, Mr Mason and Mr Painter – is engaged in a different occupation. By a strange coincidence, one is a carpenter, one a mason and one a painter; but their names do not necessarily match their trades.

   Assuming that only one of the following four statements is true, can you work out who does what?

   Mr Carpenter is not a painter
   Mr Mason is not a carpenter
   Mr Carpenter is a carpenter
   Mr Mason is not a painter

3. A logician with some time to kill in a small town decides to have his hair cut. The town has only two barbers, each with his own shop. The logician glances into one shop and sees that it is extremely untidy. The barber needs a shave, his clothes are unkempt, his hair is badly cut. The other shop is extremely neat. The barber is freshly shaved and spotlessly dressed, his hair neatly trimmed. The logician returns to the first shop for his haircut. Why?

4. 'I guarantee,' says the pet-shop salesman, 'that this parrot will repeat every word it hears.' A customer buys the parrot but finds it will not speak a single

word. Nevertheless, the salesman has been telling the truth. Can you explain?

5. In a certain African village there live 800 women. Three per cent of them are wearing one earring. Of the other 97 per cent, half are wearing two earrings, half are wearing none. How many earrings altogether are being worn by the women?

6. Two trains are 100 miles apart. They are moving towards each other, one at 40 mph, the other at 60 mph. A plane flying backwards and forwards between the two trains is travelling at 80 mph. How far does the plane fly before the trains meet?

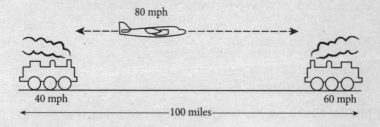

WORK BACKWARDS

Often the desired end is clear: the problem is simply how to get there. Use your imagination to visualize that end state, and then work backwards step-by-step using the logical method. This can be called future perfect thinking – when an event yet to happen is treated as if it was over. Over the page I have set out a problem scenario that tests these skills, along with an explanation of how to arrive at the solution. Once you've grasped the principle, try the similar problem titled 'Think it through 1.'

Problem

Two girls and a woman want to sail to an island. Their boat holds either the two girls or the woman. If all are competent sailors, how can they get to the island in as few trips as possible?

Solution

Visualize that end state. If you work backwards from that first trip, you begin to see that someone has to bring the boat back from the island. Thus the two girls must sail over. One girl will remain on the island while the other sails the boat back. And the rest of the problem simply requires keeping track of where everyone is at a given time.

Now test your own skills.

Think it through 1

Martha has to get her two babies, Sara and Roger, as well as the family cat, out to the car. Because Martha has a broken arm, she can carry only one baby or the cat at a time.

Unfortunately, neither child can be left alone with the cat. Sara pulls the cat's tail, causing general havoc, and the cat sheds fur on Roger's brown clothes. How does she get everyone to the car in as few trips as possible?

The answer is on p. 177.

ORGANIZE THE FACTS

A logical approach is inseparable from rearranging the information available. A problem is often a jumble of information that needs to be:

- Separated into its component parts.
- Re-arranged or restructured.

A problem is often a solution in disguise.

As you may have discovered when you tackled the exercise on p. 15, making charts or matrixes – a branch of thinking visually with your pen as a tool, rather than in your head – is a vital supporting strategy. Again, I have set out a scenario below, demonstrating how the systematic organization of facts can produce results. It is followed by an explanation of how this form of thinking works in this specific case. Once you've grasped the principle, try Think It Through 2.

Problem

Anne, Heather and Theresa live next door to each other. Heather has the flat in the middle. They work as a chemist, a radio announcer and a doctor, but not necessarily in that order. The announcer walks Theresa's dogs when Theresa goes away on holiday. The chemist taps on Anne's wall when Anne's stereo is too loud. What career does each woman have?

Solution

Try sorting out the given information in a systematic way. Make a chart to spell out every option and look for clues with which to eliminate the options one at a time. If the announcer walks Theresa's dog, then Theresa is not the announcer. The chemist taps on Anne's wall, indicating that Anne is not the chemist. So cross out those possibilities.

Reread the problem to find less obvious clues and implications. The chemist – since it isn't Anne – must be either Heather or Theresa. But Theresa cannot tap on Anne's wall – Heather's flat is in the middle. So Heather must be the chemist. Theresa, since she is neither the radio announcer nor the chemist, can only be the doctor. Anne must therefore be the radio announcer.

Now test your own skills.

Think it through 2

In a plane flying to London, five passengers are seated in a row next to each other. Their professions are journalist, singer, teacher, naval captain and engineer. They are of the following nationalities: English, French, German, Italian, Dutch. They are various ages (21, 24, 32, 40 and 52). The passengers take part in various sports (handball, swimming, volleyball, athletics and football). Their destinations in England are London, Birmingham, Manchester, Newcastle and Plymouth.

1 The engineer is seated on the extreme left.
2 The volleyball player is seated in the middle.
3 The Englishman is a journalist.
4 The singer is 21.
5 The teacher's sport is swimming.
6 The naval captain is travelling to Plymouth.
7 The handball player is French.
8 The passenger from Holland is bound for Birmingham.
9 The passenger bound for London is 32 years old.

10 The athlete is bound for Newcastle.

11 The passenger from France is seated next to the German.

12 The 40-year-old passenger is seated next to the passenger who is bound for Manchester.

13 The 24-year-old passenger is seated next to the passenger who is travelling to Birmingham.

14 The engineer is seated next to the Italian.

15 The passenger on the extreme right is older than the passenger from Holland.

     a) How old is the Naval Captain?
     b) What is the nationality of the football player?

(Time allowed: 20 minutes)

The answers are on p. 177.

THE LOGIC OF THE SITUATION

Most situations requiring an answer or a decision have a form of logic in them. Although this bears some relation to the logic of the philosophers, it is essentially a rather different sort of logic that is much more recognizable to leaders or managers.

Logic in this sense is the inevitable or predictable consequence when you add up the factors in a situation. If you are in a car speeding at one hundred miles per hour and you hit another car travelling at the same speed, the logic of the situation is that you are going to be killed or very seriously injured.

Appealing to the logic of the situation is pointing to something that forces a decision that is separate from, or even in opposition to, your own or other people's inclinations. The logic of war, for example, might compel you as a general to burn a town or shell a city.

Because logic in this sense can be used to justify such extraordinary actions it is important to subject these kinds of arguments to especially searching scrutiny. The logic of physical laws, such as gravity or motion, is in a different class to the logic derived from so-called economic, social and psychological laws. You need to distinguish between empirical observations of cause-and-effect, which gives you a sense of the logic of situations, and reasoning from theories about general situations, which is a different and more academic kind of logic.

To summarize, logical thinking is only a small part of effective thinking. It is a main branch of the analysing family, with an established and respectable offspring in the mathematical and physical sciences. But there are occasions when you have to think logically as a manager, either deductively or inductively. You will certainly need to draw the proper logical conclusions from situations. Be able to reason by taking steps down a logical path when that sort of thinking is needed. It is an important route to the truth.

SIGNPOST

At this point you have an option. You can either tackle another exercise in analytical and logical thinking, The Missing Space Rocket (below), or you can move on to Chapter 4. If you have taken more than 10 minutes on the 'Think it through' exercises above, I recommend you choose the first option.

EXERCISE 7: The missing space rocket
This exercise is designed to test your ability to cut through waffle and reach the nub of the matter. What is

essential information and what is not? Then you have to decide on your priorities. What is important and what is not? What is possible and what is not? In other words, you must analyse the situation and decide how you are going to handle it.

Put your plan for solving this problem on paper, giving your reasons, before checking against my answer on p. 180. You should complete the exercise in 30 minutes.

You are one of a small group of young team leaders working for various United Nations agencies. You have secured funding for an expedition to build a school in a remote part of Ethiopia and you are proceeding there by cargo boat. You are using some of your annual leave. Some days out of port from Cape Town and after some very rough weather, you are enjoying a walk on deck when you notice that the ship has suddenly changed course. You have hardly noted this when you are asked to go at once to the Captain's cabin where you find the Captain, his radio operator and your seven colleagues awaiting you. The Captain then gives you all the following information:

'Ladies and gentlemen, my Radio Officer has just brought me a message – a FLASH signal from the authorities at Cape Kennedy requesting immediate assistance. Before you ask any questions let me tell you that the request has United Nations Special Operations approval; and I have now to give you the following details.

'A new and secret rocket, containing a special nose cone relating to UN research into climate warming, was fired from the UN Research Space Agency Centre in Kenya a short while ago. Initially it behaved well, then deviated, and efforts to destroy it by radio signals failing, it continued its flight, but on a new course. The experts cannot understand this and say that it is impossible unless another control has taken over. They have no other controls operating, which implies that an unfriendly state has been able to redirect the flight of the rocket by means of instruments in a very high altitude aircraft, submarine, or elsewhere. Whatever the system, the rocket has now landed, but not at its correct destination.

'Its signals lasted long enough for the experts to pick up its direction, and, with its known fuel range, they are satisfied that it has landed on an uninhabited island less than 70 nautical miles from our present position. My chart shows that the island is quite small and shaped rather like a shoe with its toe pointing westwards. It has a rocky coastline, with sandbanks or reefs running out in some places as much as 10 kilometres, except on the north east coast, which, however, has steep cliffs and high ground up to 500 metres.

'Now to the main point; you have been ordered to find the cone and to ensure its safety at all costs until 09.00 hrs tomorrow, when UN security agents will arrive and take over responsibility. The cone is approx 3 metres high and 1 metre in diameter at the base. It is painted yellow with two luminous patches 1 metre square. It is not radioactive.

'I have altered course, the ship is going at full speed and we shall arrive off the island in under six hours. Now, Gentlemen, the rest is up to you.'

In reply to questions the Captain answers:

'I can give you two small boats, without engines, each with ample room for six people and three boxes of stores. We have sufficient oars but with the present sea, no small boat will make more than 2 mph, and that will be hard work. Swimming, even for a powerful swimmer, will be quite out of the question for the next 36 hours. Yes, you can have as much food and water and clothing as you want. We have equipment such as compasses, cooking utensils and torches etc., but there are only eight torch batteries each with 3 hours of reasonable life. The only cover I can offer you against possible bad weather are a couple of tents, rather old-fashioned and heavy, but in good condition and absolutely waterproof. From the ship's armoury you can take a flare gun, shot guns, and as much ammunition as you think you will require.

'Here is a sketch map prepared from my chart, which you may keep and which I hope will be useful to you. I must point out that the contours, which, as you know, are drawn at vertical intervals at specific heights above sea-level, have, in this sketch, been shown at vertical intervals of 30 metres. The island consists of volcanic rock, and, because of its rough and uneven surface, is likely to be hard going except along the south coast where there is level ground.'

You leave the cabin with the other seven team leaders and go to the dining room to study and discuss the problem. Half-an-hour later the Captain joins you and says that he has received the following further information.:

'A small unidentified submarine, possibly belonging to a country known to want to dominate global warming research for its own commercial ends, has been reported south of the island, moving north. It submerged quickly on being seen, but, if it continues on its present course, should arrive off the island at sunset. There are only three known areas along the coast where even a small boat could land, but a channel runs from one of them that would enable a submarine to get within 400 metres of the beach. This is off the north east coast; elsewhere a submarine would have to lie off 3 kilometres.

'Next, the experts at UN headquarters in New York have produced the following data, as a result of rechecking their calculations in an endeavour to pin-point the area of the cone. The cone is lying in the south-east area of the island, some 100–200 metres above sea-level, about 2 kilometres inland and on a slope that faces west. They apologize for not doing better, but say that this information can be accepted as accurate. You will observe that the possible landing areas have been marked on the sketch map and have been given names. The authorities are now satisfied that you will not be the only people searching for the cone, and that you must at all costs find and protect the nose cone.

'The only way from the landing area at Heel is by scaling the cliffs which are 200 metres high. There is a risk, but it can be done. I have some rope aboard but no other climbing gear. You should reckon on it taking you about an hour to climb those cliffs. The cone did not disintegrate on landing. That is all I have to say. Any further questions? No? Then I will leave you to it. Good luck! There is just one other point; I have been ordered to move north west from the area once you have left the ship. The time is now 09.00 hrs. Any questions?'

Some further points you discover during discussions are:

All timings have been given in GMT.

Against his training and natural inclinations, the Captain kindly converted all speeds to mph.

The bad weather you have been experiencing was due to spring gales, but the weather is clearing; visibility is good although it will be very cold at night.

The moon is in the last quarter; sunrise is at 07.00 hrs and sunset at 18.45 hrs.

The known landing areas are marked on the map and the ship can drop you either two miles off Toe, half a mile off Heel or seven miles off Arch.

The route along the south coast is good and with luck you could average 4 mph. Movement elsewhere on the island would be 3 mph.

Providing you can make your plan by 10.00 hrs and inform the Captain, he can get to any of the positions off the landing areas by 14.00 hrs and subsequently to another position by 15.30 hrs.

It is known that the type of small submarine reported carries one small landing boat capable of holding up to six persons.

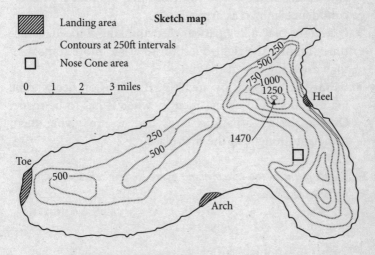

Sketch map of The Missing Space Rocket Island

KEY POINTS: ANALYSING

- To improve your decision making capability you need to become a clear thinker. Can you call to mind three people you have met who had or have a reputation for their clear thinking?

- The way to improve your skills as a clear thinker is to challenge al that appears to be – in your own thinking or in the thought of others – sloppy, inconclusive, blurred, confused, doubtful, foggy, fuzzy, muddled, obscure, unclear, unintelligible, vague. You won't be short of work!

- There is a link between having a good analytical mind and being a clear thinker. You have to be able to reduce a complex problem or situation to its essentials.

- What you need is the ability to think for yourself, as if from first principles. That requires a balance of confidence and humility: confidence in your own intellectual powers and humility that keeps you from that fatal form of over-confidence known as arrogance.

- Questions play a key part in clear thinking. Indeed, sometimes finding the right question to ask is more important than anything else at the time.

- Beware of 'paralysis by analysis'. If a decision needs to be made you should always identify when it has to be made. Over-analysing situations is as bad as not giving them sufficient thought in the first place.

He who thinks too much about every step he takes will stay on one leg all his life.

　　　　　　　　　　　　　　　　　　　　　　　Chinese proverb

4

HOLISTIC THINKING

**'The most original man is the one who
borrows from the most sources'**
Japanese proverb

In Chapter 1 the second family of mental aptitudes were called the synthesizers, because synthesis is literally the opposite to analysis. But I have reservations about the term. I cannot forget such phrases as 'synthetic rubber' or 'synthetic dyes', so the word has overtones of the artificial or man-made. Moreover, the logicians – those supreme analysts – have also taken it over to stand for deductive reasoning, or for the dialectic combination of thesis and antithesis into a higher stage of truth (the key idea that Marx borrowed from the philosopher Hegel). But synthesis can be rescued for a wider use. It essentially means the composition or combination of parts or elements to form a whole. The synthesist has a different mind set to the analyst.

Another word that can be used to describe this rather more mysterious kind of thinking is 'holistic'. In 1927 Field Marshal Jan Smuts, a keen agricultural scientist as well as a soldier and a statesman, published a book entitled *Holism and Evolution*. Holism was the word he coined to describe the tendency in Nature to produce wholes by ordering or grouping various units together. The essential realities in Nature, so Smuts wrote, are these irreducible wholes. They cannot be analysed into their parts without losing this holistic quality. His neologisms – holism and holistic – have now entered our language.

Anybody who has responsibility for the affairs of an organization – whether their title is chief executive, general manager, president or managing director – has to take a holistic view of it. Indeed, holistic thinking is the key to strategic thinking, in any field.

I used the adjective 'mysterious' about holistic thinking quite deliberately, for we cannot analyse holism very far. If we could, it would cease to be an equal partner in the triumvirate of the mind and become subordinate to the already overmighty analysing faculty. But we can coast around it, mapping one or two distinctive features. You should be aware, however, that there is a potential tension or even civil war in the human mind between analysis and holistic thinking, of which I shall give two examples presently.

THE HOLISTIC VISION

Another word that has worked well as a label for this box of mental attitudes and faculties is 'system'. We are surrounded by systems, wholes that are made up of interacting parts while somehow transcending them.

Look at a candle flame. Why does it keep approximately the same size and shape while it's flickering? In this case, the 'parts' are flows of vaporized wax, oxygen and burnt gases – the processes of combustion and diffusion give the interaction between these flows – and these interactions show us at what size and shape the flame will be approximately stable.

The strength of a rope is another example of a holistic property. This strength is a result of interaction among the individual strands, caused by twisting. With the strands untwisted. the rope's strength is governed by the weakest strand: twisted, the strands act together and increase their strength.

A holistic mind therefore has a special way of looking at things or people, at the world itself. It is not eager to take things to bits at first glance. Rather, it waits to see the full pattern, the whole – the wood rather than the trees. Equal mental weight is given to the whole in relation to the parts, hence a certain reluctance to dismember. If a nasty schoolboy pulls the legs and wings off a fly he is left with a dead fly: the parts are there but the whole is gone.

Thinkers such as Einstein exemplify this union of formidable powers of analysis with a strain of holistic thinking that seeks out the simple or whole. Werner Heisenberg, one of the fathers of quantum physics, once spoke to Einstein of the 'almost frightening simplicity and wholeness of the relationships which nature suddenly spreads out before us'. This theme of simplicity, wholeness and beauty – revealed through mathematical formula or detailed experimentation – recurs again and again as Nature's mysteries are explored. Whether that simplicity and wholeness is 'really' there or whether it is a projection of the holistic human mind, is an important question that we shall touch on later.

SOME HOLISTIC APPROACHES

Holistic thinkers prefer to deal with wholes. They tend to dislike overmuch analysis, feeling no compulsive desire to take things or people to bits to see what they are made of.

They sense that the whole is always more than the sum of its parts. They see the wood and not the trees. Latent holists can therefore appear uninterested or even hostile to an academic approach where they sense there may be an excessive emphasis on analysing.

Psychology is a good example of a subject that became excessively analytical at one stage. It became dominated by aping the natural scientist analysers around the turn of the last century. These people analysed all human experience into its sensory elements. The more holistic thinkers then counter-attacked. The Gestalt school of psychology emerged in reaction, basing itself on the following principles:

- An intuitive grasp of the overall significance of behaviour is more desirable than a precise but mechanistic explanation.
- We should try to understand relationships between events, not just events themselves.
- No event occurs in isolation, but only in a context or field that gives it significance.

You can see the holistic tendency of mind in these statements above. For the Gestalt psychologists stressed the tendency of the mind to perceive situations as a whole, rather than as several isolated elements or sensations. *Gestalt* is the German word for form or shape, organized wholes in which each part affects every other part. A melody is more than its separate notes.

The Gestalt school was labelled anti-analytic. It was not in fact against all types of analysis, but its members sensibly held that the level of analysis used should always be appropriate to the nature of reality.

A more contemporary example is the holistic movement in medicine, which works on the following principles:

- Mind and body are a unity and should be treated as such. Human imagination and the power of the unconscious mind, in particular, need to be taken seriously in medicine.
- Nature heals, we help. Thus holistic medicine looks to ancient and unconscious forces that are vital to our unity with Nature.
- What works with one person may not necessarily work with another. Medicine should be holistic – related to the person's heredity, personality, environment and lifestyle.

With orthodox medicine tending to be more materialistic and with specialization leading to an increasing concentration on symptoms rather than people, these principles behind 'alternative medicine' make good sense, even though the application of them calls for practical sense informed by experience.

THINKING HOLISTICALLY ABOUT PROBLEMS

People who don't seem to be able to think holistically tend to take a narrow view of problems, often interpreting them in single disciplinary or functional ways. 'This is a selling problem,' one might say; another, looking at the same phenomenon, might call it 'a production problem'. Sometimes such people are merely seeing a facet of the whole, not the whole itself. Consider the story below.

A small soft drinks company had been pursuing an aggressive expansion policy for several years by continuously adding new flavours to the product range. The chief executive was satisfied with the results, which showed that the volume of sales had risen quite sharply since the policy had been introduced; the sales force saw their commissions rising nicely and were pleased too. The only apparent limit to this growth was the difficulty of finding acceptable new flavours. A small laboratory was set up to research the problem.

One more immediate cause for concern had developed. The production department was finding it difficult to keep costs down to the anticipated level. In short, productivity was falling as total output went up. The managing director asked the production manager to solve that problem.

Productivity had been defined as 'the volume of output per employee hour' and the production manager found that the hours worked on the shop floor had risen much faster than total output over the period in question. So, as a first step, he introduced a productivity bonus scheme. This had only a limited effect. After a few months the trade union representative began to complain that everyone was working harder for no real benefit.

The next solution to try was reorganizing the workflow. Productivity improved, but only marginally. The installation of a new high-speed automatic bottling machine did appear to solve the problem. Soon, however, productivity began to fall again. By now the production manager realized the nub of the problem lay in the fact that each time a new flavour was made, the production line had to be stopped for cleaning. Many flavours were made in very small batches so that down time was actually greater than productive time. The greater the number of flavours produced the less time there was for production.

The production manager took a decision: he announced that he was going in for production planning on a four-week cycle. Each flavour would be manufactured only once a month. To do this effectively the sales people had to forecast the demand for each flavour the following month – an exercise they were reluctant to undertake. The chief executive intervened to get it underway. The outcome was highly pleasing for everyone until the firm began to run short of cash. Stocks of soft drinks that were being overproduced were building up and left to stand in the stores for weeks rather than days.

Finally, the chief executive called a meeting of all senior staff to discuss the situation. During it the accountant suggested that the firm stopped selling the ten least popular flavours. For the total time saved on the shop floor would, when expressed in money terms, exceed the loss of income. *The business would be better off without them.* The problem was not a production problem, nor a marketing problem, nor a stock-control problem, nor a matter of industrial relations or capital investment; it was a general management problem. To separate it into bits was misguided. Looking at the problem holistically led the managers to adopt the right solution.

NATURE AND GROWTH

Nature, wholeness and growth are all key ideas for the holistic mind. Far from being an artificial or man-made activity, synthesis is the central natural process. Breaking down wholes into their parts – that decaying tree trunk in your garden – are only preludes to a series of syntheses. When we synthesize consciously – putting together elements into a compound – we are only palely imitating what Nature is doing all the time. Because we are part of Nature, however, that natural process of growth can happen inside our minds as well as our bodies. *Ideas can start as seeds and then grow.*

This notion of ideas growing is important to holistic thinkers and may make them reluctant to submit ideas to early analysis by themselves or others. A new born baby is a whole. It grows. But in the first days of its life it needs protection from the chill winds.

Another related distinguishing characteristic of holistic

thinkers is that they make considerable use of the *story* method of understanding. They like to know how it began and how it developed.

Holistic thinking, then, is as relevant to the manager as it is to the artist, doctor or scientist. The capacity to think about organizations and teams, opportunities and problems as wholes is extremely important. You can even think holistically about a budget or a balance sheet if you are gifted that way.

Would you say you are a holistic thinker? You can certainly develop holistic thinking by becoming more aware of its importance and by deliberately refraining from analysis beyond a certain point. Let the whole take shape in your mind's eye.

SIGNPOST

There are several routes that lead from here. Chapter 4 deals with imagination, a rather more distant relative of the holistic family.

Chapter 5 looks at intuition, which involves holistic thinking done at depth mind level.

In Chapter 11, you will notice the theme emerging again in the discussion of creative thinking. Be on the alert for the holistic perspective even if the words *holistic* and *synthetic* are not used.

KEY POINTS: HOLISTIC THINKING

- An analytical mind is diametrically opposite to a holistic mind. The former separates wholes into their constituent parts. That works well with inanimate objects, with all except in the case of living beings. Then, as Wordsworth said, 'we murder to dissect'.

- Knowing how to think holistically – to see the wood as well as the trees, to see the whole that is a sum of more than the constituent parts – is a key skill for an effective thinker.

- Those who are good judges of people tend to have more holistic minds. People may have sets of qualities or strengths and weaknesses, but a psychological analysis of their traits seldom gives you a sense of knowing them. You are always dealing with a whole person.

- A baby is a whole and grows. Holistic minds, I think, tend to be attracted to growth. They like to help individuals and teams, organizations and communities, even nations, to grow to their full potential.

- Are you holistically minded? Here is a simple test. If you are trying to understand a complex social situation, do you prefer someone to analyse it for you? Or is the gateway of understanding for you the story of how the situation developed? Holistic people like to know the story behind a person or situation.

> The 'untrapped mind' is open enough to see many possibilities, humble enough to learn from anyone and everything, perceptive enough to see things as they really are, and wise enough to judge their true value.
>
> Komusuke Matsushita

5

IMAGINATIVE THINKING

'A man may prophesy,
With a near aim, of the main chance of things
As yet not come to life, which in their seeds
And weak beginnings, lie intreasured.'
Henry IV, William Shakespeare

Successful chief executives rate imagination high on the list of attributes they value most. But what is imagination and how does it contribute to business success? This chapter seeks to answer those questions and to enable you to develop your own imaginative powers.

As a rule', wrote Kenneth Grahame, author of *The Wind in the Willows*, 'grown-up people are fairly correct on matters of fact; it is the higher gift of imagination that they are so sadly to seek.'

Imagination almost certainly belongs to the family of synthesizers. Neither the analyst nor the critic is necessarily imaginative, but the synthesist is likely to be.

There is definitely a family relationship between imagination and holistic thinking. Take as an example this description of the crucial phase in composition by one of the world's great composers, Wolfgang Amadeus Mozart:

First bits and crumbs of the piece come and gradually join together in my mind; then the soul getting warmed to the work, the thing *grows* more and more, and I spread it out broader and clearer, and at last it gets almost finished in my head, even when it is a long piece, so that I can see the *whole* of it at a single glance in my mind, as if it were a beautiful painting or a handsome human being; in which way I do not hear it in my imagination at all as a succession – the way it must come later – but all at once as it were. It is a rare feast. All the *inventing* and *making* goes on in me as in a beautiful strong dream. But the best of all is the hearing of it all at once.

I have put key words or phrases in italics to emphasize the proximity of the two concepts of holistic and imaginative work in this particular passage.

Some imaginative thinkers, such as Nobel Prize winner Sir Lawrence Bragg, who pioneered X-ray crystallography, have the ability to imagine things in three dimensions in their minds. Nikola Tesla, an extremely productive technological innovator (fluorescent lights, the AC generator, the 'Tesla' coil), apparently had extraordinary powers of visualization. According to his biographer Tesla 'could project before his eyes a picture complete in every detail, of every part of the machine. These pictures were more vivid than any blueprint'. Further, Tesla claimed to be able to test his devices mentally, by having them run for weeks – after which time he would examine them thoroughly in his mind for signs of wear.

THINKING IN PICTURES

Our minds have a fundamental visual capacity: we not only see things but we can shut our eyes and remember the picture of what we have seen.

That is one pole of the imagination. In the piece quoted on the previous page, Mozart said 'I can see the whole of it at a single glance in my mind, as if it were a beautiful painting or a handsome human being'. What he saw was something that had not existed before. Imagination for him was the spearhead of inventing and making. That gives us the other pole of the imagination. But there are other shades of these abilities as well.

The table below, 'Imaginative abilities of the mind,' shows the remarkable range of our imaginative abilities, from memory function at one end of the scale to creative imagination at the other. 'Fantasy' is practices such as brainstorming, which is often taught on management courses.

Answer the questions posed below and reflect on whether you imagine in colour and in three-dimensions. Does your imagination have real thrust and life – can it get you off the runways of perceived reality?

IMAGINATIVE ABILITIES OF THE MIND	
FACTS	**ABILITIES**
Recalling	The ability to bring back an idea to mind something not actually present to the senses, such as your house or car.
Visualizing	The ability to form a picture of something not experienced in its entirety, such as what it would be like for you to walk on the moon.
Creating	The ability to form an image or whole of something actually non-existent at present, such as a new product.
Foreseeing	The ability to see a development or outcome before it materialises.
Fantasy	The ability to invent the novel and unreal by altering or combining the elements of reality in a particularly unrestrained and extravagant way.

HOW IMAGINATIVE ARE YOU?

Put YES or NO in each box

Can you recall visually with great accuracy? Imagine your last holiday and see how much detail you can see in the mental pictures. ☐

Would you describe yourself as good at visualizing things you haven't directly experienced yourself? Could you, for example, accurately imagine what it would be like to be a member of the opposite sex? Or prime minister? Or your own secretary? ☐

Has anyone praised you for your imagination within the last year? ☐

Have you invented or made anything recently, at work or in leisure time, that definitely required imagination? ☐

Do you tend to foresee accurately what happens before the event? ☐

Do you fantasize about your work or career? ☐

Do you paint or draw? ☐

Do you find it easy to choose colour schemes when you have to redecorate your room? ☐

Do you find that you can think up names for such things as babies, pets, houses? ☐

Have you ever written a story or poem? ☐

Using your imagination 1

1 Imagine you are climbing Everest by yourself and without oxygen. You are 1,000 metres from the summit.
   (a) Sit down and make a meal for yourself. Work through each of your five senses to complete the scene in your mind.

(b) You are now pressing on to the summit. What can you see? What are you touching? What are your feelings? What colours can you see?

(c) Now you are on the summit. You have a camera with you. Set it up on a rock. Stand back. Now compose in detail the photograph you have taken. Turn it into a three-dimensional picture.

2 A new creature has been discovered in the jungles of South America that is destined to replace the dog and cat as our most popular domestic pet. Briefly describe it in 200 words and draw a picture of it. Give it a name.

3 Morwenstow is a small village on the north Cornwall coast. One Sunday evening during the Napoleonic Wars the vicar was preaching at evensong in the village church. A great storm raged outside. Suddenly the congregation heard a great crash. A vessel had struck the rocks. Everyone rushed out of the church and with the vicar at their head they hurried down the steep path to the bay. In the dusk they saw the smashed wreck of a three-masted schooner, its debris scattered on the beach. There was apparently only one survivor lying unconscious on the sand. He was a swarthy man, dressed in a sea captain's uniform. But when they turned him over a look of terror came over the vicar's face . . .

Now continue the story.

You may find it fanciful to be asked to compose a short story. But there is a link between the imagination of an author and that of a businessman: both are growing something from small seeds. So don't be put off attempting the above practice exercise because it seems to have nothing to do with management.

THINKING AND IMAGINATION

It is helpful to stress the pictorial dimension of imagination but, beyond a certain point, it is better to use the word in a much broader sense. Tolstoy's *War and Peace*, which has no pictures, is a much greater work than comics, which are full of them. Avoid getting too hooked on trying to see or make mental pictures: you can think imaginatively without them. Equally you can imagine without thinking.

Let me give you an example. A mother, anxious when her child has not come home from school, imagines all sorts of scenes. She is the passive prey of horrible fantasies, which come into her mind successively in a way she cannot control. Emotion and imagination have joined forces. Her imagination is hyperactive and her powers of thinking unexercised. She is panic-stricken. In this situation thought and imagination are diametrical opposites.

In other situations we are inclined to distinguish them as just being different. For example, if you read a scientific account of the geography of northern Greenland you might be thinking analytically about the climate, flora and fauna, while also trying to visualize what the country looks like and what life might be like there. You will be thinking like a physical geographer while also composing a scenario for yourself in your imagination.

But there is a third group of situations in which a person's thinking and imagination are really inseparable, and the thinking is imaginative. Take the good detective or a top-class manager. In trying to work out problems they need to be both fertile in imagining feasible hypotheses and also careful about their data and what can be properly deduced. They must think imaginatively, but also in a coherent, methodical and unfanciful way.

Why, then, hasn't imagination been given its proper place in management training and education? First, we are still inclined to treat arithmetical computation – the sort of thing computers do – as the most characteristic exercise of the highly trained mind. I don't know where this assumption comes from. Computation, though very important, is a comparatively low form of thinking, increasingly delegated now to machines. Adding and subtracting, multiplying and dividing, hardly give much scope for originality, flair, talent, horse sense, intuition, judgement or constructiveness.

Second, we find it hard to rid ourselves of the assumption that imagination is exercised only in dreaming up fictional things or happenings. William Shakespeare declared that 'imagination bodies forth the forms of things unknown'. He did invent a living world of fictional characters and incidents. But Leonardo da Vinci and Thomas Edison had good imaginations too. Prospero and Hamlet are imaginary people, but the submarine and helicopter, the electric light bulb and telephone are not imaginary objects, though it needed a combination of imagination and technical knowledge to invent them.

Using your imagination 2

Einstein imagined how the world would look if you travelled on the back of a sunbeam. The question had first occurred to him as a child and in adulthood he acquired the intellectual equipment and knowledge to answer it. List three imaginative questions of this kind – involving fantasy – that could revolutionize familiar concepts in your working environment.

IMAGINATIVE THINKING IN ACTION

Imaginative thinking is not limited, however, to inventing things. The detective or the manager are usually not inventing or making anything but they are still thinking imaginatively. They are also linked in that they both have an adversary – the criminal in one case and competitors in another. Sportsmen and soldiers share that factor as well.

Again, let's look at an example. When a famous football player is being praised for playing imaginatively, he is not being praised for fantasizing in his armchair or writing novels about football. Rather, he is seen to do things such as the following:

- In trying to get past the opposing player he doesn't use the same jink or swerve time after time – or he may do so three times just in order to surprise his opponent on the fourth occasion with a different change of direction.
- He doesn't assume that his team mate will pass out to the right, as he did the last five times – he is ready for it to come to him this time.
- He quickly realizes a gap is likely to open up where, at the moment, no gap can be seen.

In other words, he is quick to anticipate, to see and act upon things that are out of the ordinary. He surprises his opponents and yet is not taken by surprise. He exploits the unexpected and the lack of routine.

This imaginative thinking on the football field has nothing to do with whether or not the player concerned writes fictional stories about football. It also has nothing to do with the rational and logical thinking prized so highly by the academics. Ron Greenwood, as manager of the England football team, said that 'football is a battle of wits' for which a combination of physical and mental attributes is needed:

> A football brain is quite different from an academic brain. I coached at Oxford University for seven years and if the students had had the right kinds of football brains they would have been the best team in the world. But they didn't and they weren't. A man who can hardly read or write can have a great football brain.

Imagination of a kind also helps the criminal. The following parable illustrates that imagination, together with the entrepreneurial spirit, can flourish, in the most limiting circumstances. Consider this story:

Bernard Leach had a worldwide reputation as a potter, and his pots were selling for hundreds, and in some cases thousands, of pounds, with public auction rooms keen to cash in on the wave of popularity. Two prisoners in Featherstone Prison near Wakefield in Britain were quick to realize the implications for them. They were attending pottery classes and set about copying Leach's work from photographs in books and magazines. On one occasion they impressed the prison authorities by their enthusiasm for the craft by making 14 'Leach' pots. Even more significantly, a Bernard Leach 'seal', BL, was stamped on to the base of the wares.

Prisoners are not allowed to sell the pots they make, but can pay a nominal charge of a few pence per item and give them to friends and family. The potters handed their pots to an antique dealer friend, who duly placed them for sale at London auction houses, including Christie's, where they sold for prices of over £1,000 each. Their only mistake was to put too many on to the market too quickly. After they were caught, one of the three prisoners explained that he had put BL on the pots because one of his aliases was Bernard Lee!

Imaginative thinking of this kind is clearly relevant to fields other than criminal forgery in prison, detective work or football. War, for example, calls for it constantly. The fighter pilot in the Battle of Britain had to use his imagination as he ducked and weaved his way through interminable dogfights. Successful generals down the ages have shown the same capacity. Winston Churchill once wrote:

> Nearly all the battles which are regarded as the master-pieces of the military art have been battles of manoeuvre in which very often the enemy has found himself defeated by some novel device, some unexpected thrust or strategy. In such battles the losses of the victor have been small and the enemy is left puzzled as well as beaten.

In business your next move is not blueprinted for you. It's true, you don't have total freedom. You don't have the freedom of, say, someone writing a television script or the composer of a poem. But you are like a person crossing an unmapped plateau. You have to think up for yourself and then experimentally try out possible ways of getting where you want to be – and the solutions to these problems are not in books, nor can they be recalled from your memory bank. For you have never been here before. You have to originate or innovate, and you cannot innovate by following established precedents or by applying common recipes. John Sainsbury, former chairman of the chain of British supermarkets that bears his family name, once said:

The characteristic in a good manager which I appreciate almost above all else is that of imagination. The good manager has to be imaginative in order to be a successful innovator. Success in that respect brings not only a valuable contribution to any enterprise, but also the considerable personal satisfaction of creative achievement.

It is imagination that is needed to anticipate events and to respond to change. It is only those with a lively imagination who can really develop sensitive understanding of others, be they customers, colleagues or shop floor workers. To be able to do that is a vital ingredient of success in commerce or industry.

YES, BUT CAN YOU DEVELOP IMAGINATIVE THINKING?

We all have a capacity to synthesize. In widely differing degrees we are all inventive, For example, we make casual little jokes of our own. They may not be very witty or bring the house down, but they are new jokes and not the 'Did you hear the one about . . .?' variety. Notice, now, that if we are asked to say how we came to think of a joke we are stumped for an answer. There seems to be no technique or recap or method of joke making. So we reply vaguely, 'Oh! It just came to me.'

Yet inventive thinking, while not a matter of mere technique, is not a matter of mere luck either. You can be sure that professional comedians do research on jokes, keeping card indexes of the jokes themselves as well as their audience reactions. Perhaps people laugh at mother-in-law jokes more in some countries than others – they probably classify jokes by type in this way. They may even try to analyse and make generalizations about the concept of humour. What is it that makes people laugh? What situations are intrinsically funny? (Relationships may be of note here.) For example, humour is connected to our sense of proportion, which is why we laugh at a very large person riding a very small bicycle, or at some preposterous boast or claims the comedian makes. Humour, like creative thinking, often happens when two lines of apparently unconnected thought suddenly intersect.

Have you come across any imaginative thinking at work recently? The same principles certainly apply in the sphere of management. You may like to do some research on examples of imaginative thinking in business and to reflect upon the situations in which it is called for. These activities will not in themselves make you more imaginative but they will stimulate your interest and enrich your concept of the imaginative and resourceful manager.

Sportsmen find it helpful to imagine themselves in future situations: relaxed, confident and masterful. Imagine yourself at the next committee meeting saying, 'Look, aren't we falling into our usual rut again? Can't we be more imaginative?' Imagine the look of amazement on your colleagues' faces!

Using your imagination 3

You work for the pharmaceutical division of a multinational. You have just invented a simple cure for the common cold and the whole world will be grateful. You will become rich and famous when your discovery is confirmed, as it surely will be. Imagine the scene in the New York boardroom of your company at a reception held in your honour. See the riches you are about to acquire. If you think that such fantasizing is 'unreal' it is worth recalling that Leonardo da Vinci indulged in it while working mentally on his designs for a submarine and a machine for mass-producing needles: he pictured the fame and the untold riches that awaited him if he was successful in both enterprises.

Changing your self-image, the way you see yourself, is probably the most powerful way to unlock the doors of the practical imagination. If you don't apply imagination to yourself you are unlikely to apply it in life.

Using your imagination 4

- Do you see yourself as having an analytical mind that is sometimes imaginative, or an imaginative mind that is also analytical?
- When you visualize yourself – the concept you have of yourself – do you see or sense considerable potential waiting to be realized inside you?
- Imagine yourself in five years time as a chief executive with a proven reputation for imaginative action. How did you acquire that reputation? Create three more-or-less credible fantasies to explain your sudden emergence from the pack.

IMAGINATION IN PERSPECTIVE

Imagination should not be promoted to top place in the hierarchy of thinking abilities. It should be a team player, not the captain. It is the vanguard, the advance scouting party, of thinking. The specific role of imagination is to lead us into innovating, inventing, creating, exploring, risk-taking, and adventuring.

The leader who knowingly ventures off or beyond the

beaten track, the path of well trodden expectations, is show-ing some degree of imagination. His or her business ventures may turn out to be fruitless, random or crazy. For leaders who dream, dreams may be pathfinders, but they may also lead to the bankruptcy courts. Of those who depart from well-established ways only a few are explorers. 'Imaginative', 'inventive' and 'adventurous' are terms of praise, but equally 'fanciful', 'reckless' and 'crazy' describe those who are failed imaginative thinkers.

Be on guard, therefore, against any tendency to glorify the notion of imagination as an end in itself. People sometimes forget that a lively imagination can also be a silly one. Scope for originality is also freedom to be a crackpot. Both the genius and the crank are imaginative thinkers – some are both at the same time.

Yet imagination covers some crucial qualities in the busi-ness leader. There will be plenty of situations in your future career that will call on your powers of originating, inventing, improvising, discovering, innovating, exploring, experiment-ing, and of knowingly leaving the beaten track. Can you imagine yourself now doing all those things?

KEY POINTS: IMAGINATIVE THINKING

- Imagination is our power to form images in our minds or to picture or conceive things we cannot actually see and have not directly experienced.
- Imagination is also linked to the higher creative faculty. Here it creates new forms of reality, giving shape to things unknown or new by recombining the products of past experience.
- Creativity is about having new ideas and innovation is about turning them into improved or new products and

services. Both creativity and innovation call for imaginative thinking.

- It is imagination that is needed to anticipate events and to respond to change.
- Only those with a lively imagination can really develop sensitive understanding and empathy for others, be they team members, colleagues or customers.

Vision is the art of seeing things invisible.

Jonathan Swift

6

VALUING

'He who is a slave of truth is a free man.'
Arab proverb

Valuing is one of the three essential components in thinking. We cannot avoid it. This chapter asks you to reflect on the concept of value and, in particular, on the importance of the value of truth in decision making.

After *ability to take decisions* and *leadership*, the executive heads of British industry put *integrity* in third place in their list of twenty-five attributes. Lord Slim defined integrity by its effects: 'it is the quality which makes people trust you'. But what is it about integrity that induces that feeling?

The word itself means entireness, wholeness, soundness. It is a holistic word. You might be tempted to conclude that integrity as such does not exist; perhaps it is the pattern of all your moral qualities. For it implies a unity that indicates an independence of parts and completeness and perfection of the whole. But there are some distinctive elements. Integrity implies adherence to a code of moral, artistic or other values. It suggests, too, trustworthiness and incorruptibility to a degree that one is incapable of being false to a trust, responsibility or pledge.

At the core of integrity lies the value of truth. Its most

common synonym is *honesty*, the refusal to lie, steal or deceive in any way. These qualities of character rest on the assumption that you can perceive the truth in a situation. That ability is obviously vital to good decision making. For decision making rests on two pillars:

- Establishing the truth
- Knowing what to do

Because managers are prey to time pressures, and tend to be action-oriented anyway, they are inclined to skimp on the first and move too quickly on to the more congenial second.

THE AUTONOMY OF VALUING

To repeat an earlier point, valuing is a distinctive function. Most of us are now aware that you cannot get a value from a fact. No amount of reasoning, logical argument, emotional appeal or factual information can prove a value. Nor, as a famous phrase has it, can you get an *ought* from an *is*.

Moreover, like imagining, valuing appears sometimes to be quite separate from the reasoning processes we call thinking. The professor of botany who spends his life analysing and comparing the 250 or so varieties of buttercup in the world might suddenly spot a host of yellow buttercups blazing in an Alpine meadow and say 'How beautiful they look!' This has nothing to do with rational thought.

There are times, however, when valuing and thinking are virtually inseparable. By chance, the day before writing this chapter, I took an old telescope into Christie's auction house in London, intending to sell it. The expert at the reception desk turned it over, examined it, tapped it. 'No maker's name', he mused, as if to himself, 'but still, that need not matter.' Looking up he said, 'This brass section here would probably have been covered by leather.' More musing. 'It's worth about £30. I am afraid we cannot sell it here, because the cost of doing so would exceed our commission. Try a local saleroom.'

You can clearly see two parts or pillars of decision making here. First, the truth about the telescope and its value had to be established. That, if you like, was the first objective. Truth in this sense is an account of things as they are. The most immediate and most widely used synonym is real or reality. Reality is complex and has different levels; truth is the grasp, always partial, always subjectively conditioned, that we have of reality.

The second part was a decision based upon that appraisal. The Christie's expert had three options open to him:

- Yes, we should like to put your telescope in our next sale of optical instruments.
- No, we suggest you sell it elsewhere.
- Wait, may I do more research on it and consult my colleagues? We will let you know our decision.

In this case the expert's information about the telescope – the truth as he perceived it – led him unerringly to the second option. The preliminary work of establishing the truth, in other words, made the work of decision making effortless. In management those two distinct but related activities – thinking it out and deciding what to do – need to be held apart by a deliberate act of mind.

Thinking must precede and guide action to be effective. Yet there seems to be a lack of awareness by many executives that the effectiveness of any action – excluding luck – rests on the quality of the thinking that precedes it. From your experience do you agree?

A POLICY FOR THINKERS

Valuing is, of course, partly subjective anyway: it involves a capacity to value that we all have. But is it wholly subjective or only partly so? Do I really see the truth about that telescope or am I reading it into the thing? After all, I am told that the red pen I am writing with is not red at all – things do not have colour – it is just reflecting light in a certain way that activates my 'red' eye cells.

We obviously cannot prove the case either way, but we can get near to it. Take, for example, the mass exterminations perpetrated in concentration camps such as Belsen and . Dachau during the Second World War. Even Bertrand Russell, who held the view that truth was subjective, had to admit that evil was there, whatever the opinions of philosophers. In the minds of some beholders, however, the evil did not exist; it was an objective quality or value intrinsic to the place and the people who staffed its mass-production methods of death.

Whatever your philosophical or religious views, provided you have not come down irrevocably on the 'truth does not exist' side, I should like to persuade you to adopt a central policy as a thinker (which you probably do already, consciously or unconsciously). And that is to assume that truth exists. For that act of faith produces the best results. (The proposition that 'there are no bad followers, only bad leaders' may not be true, but it is still an excellent maxim to remember.)

The policy of behaving as if truth was an object, that we discover truth rather than invent it, has been enormously helpful in science. There is a link here with religion. Albert Einstein, who stood in the Jewish tradition, reflected that fundamental belief in the 'givenness' of truth and other values springing from the mind of some holistic 'other'. He believed, as he put it, that God might pose difficult problems but would never break the rules by posing unanswerable ones. Blind chance was never the answer: 'God does not play dice with the world'. He once described his fundamental quest for truth by saying 'I want to know how God created the world. I am not interested in this or that phenomenon, in the spectrum of this or that element. I want to know his thoughts, the rest are details.'

Einstein is an especially apt example. His theory of relativity had a profound influence. When such fundamental concepts as absolute space and absolute time were proved to be relative – one man's now is another man's then, for now is a subjective concept valid only for an observer with one specific frame of reference – it was widely believed that all values or concepts, such as truth, were equally relative. One man's truth is another man's lie – it all depends on where you stand.

This popular impression rests largely on a misunderstanding of what Einstein actually discovered. When the Archbishop of Canterbury asked Einstein to comment on the common view that his theory had altered human values, the physicist replied: 'Do not believe a word of it. It makes no difference. It is purely abstract science.' Elsewhere he wrote:

> The meaning of relativity has been widely misunderstood. Philosophers play with the word, like a child with a doll. Relativity, as I see it, merely denotes that certain physical and mechanical facts that have been regarded as positive and permanent, are relative to certain other facts in the sphere of physics and mechanics.

Scientists do not have to hold any kind of religious belief in a deity, however intangible and impersonal, to adopt the policy of believing that truth is 'out there', that it is like a quarry in a dense forest to be trapped, hunted or cornered. The community of scientists does act precisely as if that is what it believes, and the results have indeed been spectacular.

In management I suggest this same policy has more to be said for it than any other. If you act on the assumption that there is a truth 'out there' you will struggle to find it, knowing that only decisions based on truth are likely to be successful. We certainly know the converse to be true: if a decision is based on faulty evidence it is unlikely to be successful.

Ask yourself the following questions:

Can you identify a situation at work where you would be compelled to resign on grounds of conscience?

Have you ever, in your career, refused to tell a lie and borne the consequences?

Do you act as if you believe that truth is 'out there' when you are thinking?

'Truth is great and shall prevail, when none care whether it prevail or not.' Do you think that the truth has a power or life of its own: that it will assert itself if only we allow it to do so?

To summarize, valuing and values can be seen as a quite distinct and autonomous family. The capacity to value is universal. The actual values we adopt or express in action will be conditioned by society, but it does not necessarily follow that values as such do not have objective reality. That may or may not be so, depending upon the ultimate nature of the universe. But the practical belief that value is there has paid off in science. It makes you alert to look for something and not to be satisfied until you have found it. You may be sceptical but you are not cynical. You have the right attitude.

CONSULTING SPECIALISTS

When concentrating attention on that initial phase in decision making – establishing the truth – valuing is mixed in with all the other elements of thinking. You will be analysing and restructuring; you will be calling on your depth or subconscious mind for intuitions; you will be drawing heavily on your memory for relevant information or experience. But the valuing theme should be predominant.

By definition almost, as a strategic leader you are a generalist. You may not understand all the complexities of advanced finance or all the mysteries of high technology. To do the 'establishing the truth' part you will have to consult others. In the theoretical world of organizational studies these specialists and staff advisers will give you the information upon which you can base your judgement. In practice, being human, these specialists are all valuers too. They are offering their valuations – information plus a truth-judgement – just as surely as that expert at Christie's who gave me a valuation on my telescope.

This dependence on specialist help, together with valuing characteristics of those who advise us, means that we have to become adept at another form of valuing, namely discovering if our advisers are telling us the truth. This is where educated intuition comes in. Once again, the human element makes another entry on to the stage of effective decision making.

In assessing the value of the information someone is giving you, you must gauge their intellectual and professional calibre. You will always have at least a little knowledge about the matter in question, otherwise you would not be where you are. Use it to assess your adviser's more specialized knowledge. If there is an apparent conflict between what you are being told and what you sense to be the case, sort it out. Don't be afraid to ask questions that will give you a reasonably accurate idea of the length, depth, height and width of this person's knowledge. Don't make false assumptions about the other person's expertise. Have they been reliable in the past? Do they have a reputation for honesty and integrity? Can you trust them to tell you the truth, however unpalatable it may be?

Bad advisers will feed you interpretations of the situation that are far from objective or value-free. They want you to follow a particular course, and they feed you information to support their interpretation of reality. Conflicting evidence is put into the footnotes; other options are relegated to the appendices.

President Kennedy's decision in 1961 to countenance and support an invasion of Cuba by Cuban dissidents based in Florida – the Bay of Pigs affair – provides a classic example of how advisers with their own interests and objectives in mind can exercise a harmful influence on decision making. The body urging him to attempt the abortive invasion of Cuba by proxy – the Central Intelligence Agency – also happened to be the department supplying him with information about Cuba and the Cubans. You can guess what happened. This fact does not excuse Kennedy, of course. He had some knowledge from other sources, such as the newspapers. He should have made a judgement about the experts and the degree to which they could be expected to be impartial or disinterested. At least he learnt his lessons and dealt with the later Cuban missile crisis far more effectively.

In consequence a priority for anyone in a strategic leadership position should be to place a premium on being a truth-led organization. Discourage anyone who seeks to supply you with filtered or distorted information in order to support their preferred course of action. Create an atmosphere where everyone is committed to finding the truth and acting upon it. Be willing to admit that you are wrong if the truth compels you to do so. By so doing you will set a good example.

Read the following example. It is about a comparatively little known scientist called R. V. Jones in the Second World War who was called on to give specialist advice to Sir Winston Churchill. See if you can think of managers who exemplify this quality of truth-seeking in decision making, whether they are in the position of the chief executive (Churchill) or the specialist adviser (Jones).

Sir Winston Churchill always had a soft spot for what in those days were often called the 'backroom boys'. As Chancellor of the Exchequer in the 1920s he would summon Sir Ralph Hawtrey, the Treasury's financial and economic expert, with the instruction, according to his private secretary P. J. Grigg, that 'The learned man should be released from the dungeon in which we were said to have immured him, have his chains struck off and the straw brushed from his hair and clothes, and be admitted to the light and warmth of an argument in the Treasury boardroom with the greatest living master of argument.'

During his period as Prime Minister during the Second World War, Sir Winston's favourite 'boffin' – a scientist employed by the government – was a young, softly spoken scientist called Dr R. V. Jones. The Prime Minister would summon him from the headquarters of MI6 across St James Park.

Reg Jones made his great breakthrough on 21 June 1940. With his team he had been puzzling over radio beams transmitted from Germany during bomber raids over England and became convinced they were a navigation device for steering aircraft to their targets. Some senior scientists were highly sceptical, refusing to believe that beams could be bent around the earth's surface. R. V. Jones believed they could, and what is more, that they could be bent again by counter measures in order to redirect the aerial raiders away from urban areas to drop their bombs over open country.

Jones entered his office that morning to find a message instructing him to come to the Cabinet Room at No. 10 Downing Street. Suspecting revenge for a practical joke, he thought little of it but checked and found the message was genuine. He arrived twenty-five minutes late.

At one point in the meeting Churchill asked him to elaborate a point of detail. Instead he spoke for twenty minutes. 'The few minutes of desultory discussion that had ensued after my entry showed me that nobody else knew as much about the matter as I did myself,' he recalled later, 'and, although I was not conscious of my calmness at the time, the very gravity of the situation seemed to generate the steady nerve for which it called.'

Reg Jones made a lasting impression on the Prime Minister. Thereafter Churchill swore by him as 'the man who broke the bloody beam'; heady stuff for a 28-year-old.

'The first thing was to be absolutely scrupulous in trying to establish the truth,' Jones said as he recollected his meetings with Churchill. 'Winston said: "You don't have to be polite; you just have to be right." If you got somebody, however eminent, and asked him three successive 'Why's?', there were not many people who could stand up to it. It was quite astonishing how shaky their knowledge base was. It was the old story of 99 per cent perspiration and one per cent inspiration. One needed a very sound grounding in basic principles and a mistrust of elaborate argument when something simple would do.'

The standard set by both Churchill and Jones – to be absolutely scrupulous in trying to establish the truth – is a high one and calls for teamwork in any organization. But nothing less than attaining that standard should be your first aim if you seek excellence in business leadership.

VALUING IN PERSPECTIVE

Valuing is a general function of the mind: it is a dimension in all thinking rather than a self-contained function. But in certain mental situations we are conscious that it is playing the leading part, way ahead of analysing, synthesizing or imagining. It may be most evident when you are acting as a judge, criticizing someone casually, or trying to establish relative worth in a formal situation, such as interviewing someone for a job. When we say someone has good judgement this is our broad term for describing someone who is good at valuing as opposed to, say, someone who excels in logical thinking or having a fund of new ideas – not, of course, that these are mutually exclusive.

Because valuing is so general, in this chapter I have concentrated on the primacy of its truth-seeking form and your need to develop it by all means at your command. For establishing the truth – or the reality – of a situation seems to be the essential preliminary to knowing what is feasible. Decisions based on wishful thinking, false assumptions, undetected errors, careless calculations, faulty figures or vain assurances are hardly likely to succeed, except by luck.

A true leader will always speak the truth. For then his or her people will see the reality of the situation. Helping groups and organizations to do so and to respond appropriately lies at the very heart of leadership, especially in testing times. Consider the story on the following page.

La Vallete, the 72 year old Grand Master of the Knights of St John, who commanded Malta during the great siege by an immense force of Turks three centuries ago, was such a leader. Upon hearing news that there was no hope of an early relief he read this dispatch to his Council. 'We now know', Vallete said, 'that we must not look to others for our deliverance! It is only upon God and our own swords that we may rely. Yet this is no cause for us to be disheartened. Rather the opposite, for it is better to know the truth of one's situation than to be deceived by specious hopes'.

Surely La Vallete is right. But it is not always so easy to discover the truth of one's situation. The facts can be extremely complex, often distorted by others and apparently contradictory. This takes us to the mind's faculty for perceiving truth directly – intuition.

KEY POINTS: VALUING

- According to an ancient Roman proverb, 'Integrity is the noblest possession'. Integrity implies trustworthiness and incorruptibility to a degree that one is incapable of being false to a trust. A person of integrity prizes truth above all else.
- Establishing the truth – the realities of the situation or what is in fact the case – is always a necessary condition for effective decision making. Not that it is easy. Indeed, in some situations truth may be hard to come by.
- When making decisions we often need to consult specialists with the necessary professional or technical knowledge. But it is not wise to accept what they say without question.

Here is another use of your valuing skills: you need to evaluate the advice you are given by a specialist in relation to the decision in question.

- You can see now that your ability as a decision maker depends largely upon your judgement, and judgement in turn is mainly a function of your values and your valuing skills.

- For a good leader truth is not just factual accuracy – reflecting reality – although that remains important. It also means trustworthiness, reliability and straightforwardness.

Truth is the language that identifies what is universal.
                                        Antoine de St. Exupéry

7

YOUR SIXTH SENSE – INTUITION

'The truth has such a face and such a mien,
As to be loved needs only to be seen.'

John Dryden

What is intuition? How can you make better use of it? The aim of this chapter is to increase your awareness of the part played by intuition in decision making. It will also provide you with guidelines for making more effective use of your intuitive powers.

Intuition is the power or faculty of immediately appre-hending that something is the case. It apparently occurs without the intervention of any reasoning process. There is no deductive or inductive step-by-step reasoning, no con-scious analysis of the situation, no employment of the imagination – just a quick and ready insight – 'I just know'.

'I have but a woman's reason', said one of Shakespeare's heroines. 'I think him so because I think him so.' Down the centuries women have been noted for their powers of intui-tion. Men have been counted as the more logical of the two sexes. Would you agree?

The aim of intuition is usually truth in some form or

other. Therefore it is often a form of valuing done, if you like, without conscious effort and very quickly. The mind simply discerns the truth about a situation or a person, and that is it. Indeed, there is a tradition in philosophy known as intuitionalism, which holds that certain elements of knowledge – such as the fundamental principles of ethics – are based entirely upon intuition.

You recall that I suggested in the last chapter that we should distinguish between two phases in decision making:

- Establishing the truth of the matter
- Deciding what to do

The first process can be hard work. Sherlock Holmes personifies the thinker who relies primarily on looking carefully at the evidence and drawing correct deductions from the premises. That is one strategy. But the intuitive person does not seem to follow that route. His mind tells him instantly what must have happened or who committed the murder.

In practice it is not a question of either/or. A Sherlock Holmes may work logically for a time and then suddenly have an intuition, or conversely an intuitive person may be equipped with formidable powers of analysis that he habitually brings to bear upon his intuitions.

How intuitive are you?

Intuition is awareness that a situation exists when reason of logic – if consulted – might say that it was improbable or even impossible for it to do so. Do you have such awareness:

Rarely	☐	Sometimes	☐
Frequently	☐	Never	☐

In your judgement of people do you tend to rely upon first impressions? Are they usually right?

Do you often 'feel' your way to a decision or to the solution of problems?

Do you find it difficult sometimes to explain your intuitions to others?

When your intuitions turn out to be wrong, by hindsight why is this so?

Managers are often deterred from recognizing and using their own intuitive powers because they feel that, somehow, intuition is not intellectually respectable. It is certainly, they believe, not scientific enough. The cult of the rational manager has an iron grip on such minds. But this is nonsense. Some of the most celebrated scientists have been intuitive in their work. Some words by Einstein prove that point:

> There is no logical way to the discovery of these elemental laws. There is only the way of intuition, which is helped by a feeling for the order lying behind the appearance.

TRUSTING YOUR INTUITION

If you are now inclined to be more aware and to give more status to intuition in thinking you have already taken the first step towards making better use of it. The next step is to learn to trust your intuitive powers. That does not mean always, nor does it mean occasionally, because one cannot generalize about how often. But you should be prepared to give your intuition the benefit of the doubt; you should build up a warm and friendly relationship to that part of your mind which is prepared to offer you this unique service.

Intuition in practice

Read the following brief account and consider the questions:

Mrs Golda Meir, former Israeli Prime Minister, once said she caused the initial debacle in the 1973 Yom Kippur War and ruined her political career, because she ignored her own intuition.

In her autobiography, the Russian-born and American-raised woman who became Israel's Prime Minister, revealed that when, on Friday, 5 October 1973, news was received that the Russian advisers were leaving Syria in a hurry, 'I tried not to become obsessive', she wrote. 'Besides, intuition is a very tricky thing. Sometimes it must be acted upon at once, but sometimes it is merely a symptom of anxiety.'

She was reassured by Moshe Dayan, then Minister of Defence, Chief of Staff and Chief of Intelligence. They did not think war was imminent. Nor did General Bar Lev, former Chief of Staff.

She added: 'Today I know what I should have done. I should have overcome my hesitations that Friday morning. I should have listened to the warnings of my own heart and ordered a call-up. For me, that fact cannot and never will be erased and there can be no consolation in anything that anyone else has to say.'

Do you agree that Mrs Meir should have acted upon her intuition that Friday morning?

Can you identify an episode in your own life when you had an intuition which you failed to act upon? What were the consequences?

EMOTION AND INTUITION

'Sometimes it is merely a symptom of anxiety'. It is intuition that is being described here. Emotion and intuition have their sources close together in the hinterland of the brain. Indeed, they are so close that it is quite possible for the wires to be crossed. The negative emotions of fear and anxiety can express themselves as intuitions. A nervous passenger may have an intuition that his flight to Paris will crash and he transfers to another one. The success rate in these anxiety intuitions is remarkably low. Positive emotions can also lead to wishful intuitions. A man or woman in love can have intuitions about the character of the adored lover that turn out to be groundless.

One implication is that a thinker who relies heavily upon intuition – as many really effective thinkers do – must be physically and emotionally fit. You only have to have a bad bout of flu to know how it affects your emotions: you may become more irritable and more depressed; your focus of interest drops down to your tummy; you feel awful; you may be quite certain you are about to die. It is still remarkable, however, how many politicians and generals are allowed to make decisions when physically sick or mentally exhausted.

Stress and tiredness of mind or body can definitely play havoc with the intuitive thinker's immediate comprehension of the reality of a situation. Mountaineers are aware that the quality of decisions drops dramatically when taken in a state of exhaustion. If you are tired, it is best to think logically what to do, and not to rely on your intuition.

The classic example of the effects of emotional stress, physical sickness and plain tiredness on an intuitive man is the case of Adolf Hitler. Hitler had considerable flair as a politician and as a military leader. His decision to invade

France through the Ardennes was based on an intuition of the truth in contrast to the more logical thinking of his opponents and even his own highly rational General Staff. But, by 1945, the effects of war had reduced him to a shadow of his former self. Stress symptoms, such as hand trembling and face twitches, were visible to all. As he disliked bad news he surrounded himself with men who filtered information for him. Bad news was dressed up as good news. Gradually Hitler lost contact with reality and increasingly retreated into a private world, symbolized by the underground Führerbunker of his last weeks. Disturbed by stress and emotion, fed with misleading information, his intuition had become a worthless instrument.

BUSINESS FLAIR

'Looking back on my own scientific work', said Lord Adrian, a former Nobel Prize winner, 'I should say that it shows no great originality but a certain amount of business instinct which leads to the selection of a profitable line.'

Instinct, flair and intuition are really all much the same. A person who consistently deploys an instinctive power of discernment in a certain field is said to have flair. He can 'smell' a good prospect or which direction the truth might lie in; rather than reasoning towards his goal step-by-step he sniffs his way there by intuition. Indeed, flair comes from a French verb meaning 'to smell'.

Note the following comment from J. Paul Getty:

When I first started drilling in the Oklahoma oil the consensus of expert judgement held that there could be no oil in the so-called Red Beds region. But like so many oilmen, I chose to temper all 'analytical' thinking with a healthy dose of non-logical subjectivity. To me, the area looked as if it might hide oil. Largely on the basis of a hunch, I decided to see for myself. I began drilling in the Red Beds, struck oil and brought in a vast new producing field. I rather suspect that by relying upon such non-textbook thought processes and taking attendant risks, the biggest fortunes have been made – in oil and other endeavours.

Business flair is a consistent theme in the lives of great industrialists and merchants. They intuitively spot an opportunity for making money. They can smell a potential profit where others can see nothing but present losses. It is an instinct that is separate from the dictates of reason or logic that guide more plodding minds. When it is not followed, such businessmen often later realize their mistake, just as Golda Meir did.

If you add to this kind of business flair the willingness to take risks in the employment of capital, you are dealing with an entrepreneur. An entrepreneur can be a one-man operator, of course, but more often than not he sets up a company. He organizes. He becomes in effect a manager or at least an employer of managers whom he hires to run his business. But despite his gifts of intuition in business situations he might not be nearly so intuitive about people. For Nature rarely bestows all its mental talents on one person.

The career of Henry Ford provides an interesting case study of a thinker with an unusual combination of intuitive strengths. As a man he was stubborn, hard to persuade and erratic. A farmer's son in Michigan, Ford eventually achieved his goal and produced a car for the masses.

Ford had little formal education and as a result had difficulty in both reading and writing. However, he had a natural mechanical aptitude that manifested itself early on when he repaired and serviced his father's farm machinery. The arrival of the first American automobile fired his imagination and he set himself the objective of producing a motor car. This he achieved after seven years of toil – all in his leisure time. Ford was not a brilliant mechanic, but he had aptitude and burning ambition, hardworking capability and an interest in innovation.

Ford's first car, produced in 1896 when he was part owner and chief engineer of the Detroit Auto Company, proved to be a commercial failure. He was undaunted, however, and started to develop a motor car that people in their thousands would want to buy. This unique intuition was the key to Ford's success. He saw a whole brand new market for mass transport. This concept, and the determination to be 'first with the most' drove him on. It was indicative of his mind that he determined to travel down one path to the exclusion of all others. There was no pretence at being a broad thinker.

Ford was exceptionally weak in face-to-face encounters and went out of his way to avoid such confrontations. Decisions affecting his senior executives, often controversial, were never discussed. He never told people why they were fired, his totally intuitive approach often seemed at odds with reason. There is some inconsistency between his concern, on the one hand, for paying high wages, and on the other, his disregard for personal feelings if his intuition told him to do something. It was impossible to understand Ford in a logical way; he was a man who had to be sensed.

This intuitive approach did, however, provide Ford with one of his greatest strengths – his ability to detect the strengths and weaknesses of people and consequently his ability to form and reform the team around him. It was his generation of this almost perpetual revolution that kept the Ford Motor Company active. He never allowed people to be exposed for too long to the same job because he felt that this would stifle creativity. This style kept the industry in perpetual ferment but also kept it fresh with change.

By the early 1920s the Ford Motor Company was the world's biggest company, with huge cash reserves even by today's standards. By the end of that decade, though, Ford was unprofitable and uncompetitive and it stayed that way until Henry Ford's grandson Henry Ford II took over in 1944. The reasons for the dramatic decline are many: General Motors was a main cause in the market place. But the whole Ford story had become a controlled experiment in mismanagement. Henry Ford's empire almost died because his style, so right in the early days, was not appropriate when the company became a giant. Henry Ford was the 'boss'; he gave the orders, took all the decisions and his subordinates were simply not allowed to think for themselves or to manage.

SUMMARY

Far from being a marginal and out-dated quality, intuition is central to the way successful thinkers work. For the natural or applied scientist, it is the apparently unconscious ability that some individuals have to pick out from various possibilities the actual way in which a process does or could work; or it may be an early recognition from below the conscious level, that you are on the right track; yet again it may be the flair to select problems or lines of enquiry that are both important and soluble. These results matter equally to the manager in his field. Therefore encourage intuition in yourself. Become more aware of it. Be more receptive to its often faint whisper. Always subject it, however, to evaluation. Granted that safeguard, intuition can save you a great deal of time in decision making.

KEY POINTS: YOUR SIXTH SENSE – INTUITION

- Intuition is the power or faculty of immediately apprehending that something is the case. It seems to occur without any conscious reasoning.
- There is plenty of evidence that effective decision makers do listen to their intuition.
- Where strong emotions are in play intuition can be highly unreliable. Equally, physical states such as tiredness or stress can distort the mind's natural workings. But in general decision making in such low states or conditions of mind should, if possible, be avoided.
- Instinct, flair and intuition are cut from the same cloth. Flair is an instinctive power of discernment in a certain field. You can 'smell' an opportunity or the direction of the path to success.
- At its best intuition works because more information is going into your mind through your senses than your faculties at their conscious level can process. So your depth mind does some informal analysing, synthesizing and valuing, and an intuition that occurs in the conscious mind is one of its products.
- If an intuition comes to you after a longish period of time it is likely to be more reliable; if it comes very early in the story, take your time in checking it out.

While the fisher sleeps the net takes the fish.
                                        Ancient Greek proverb

8

YOUR DEPTH MIND

'There is a great deal of unmapped country within us.'
English proverb

The previous chapter on intuition highlighted the importance of the depth or unconscious mind's part in thinking. This chapter continues on that theme, relating it specifically to business decisions. It has the specific objective of helping you to make better use of what might be called your mental computer.

Have you ever had the experience of locking up your house and setting out on a journey, only to remember after a mile or two that you have left a light on, or a window open, or forgotten some vital piece of paper? Most of us have. We call it memory, but it is not the same sort of memory we rack when trying to recall someone's name when asked or, say, the name of some product that is now unavailable.

If you think about it, your mental computer has to scan and process an enormous amount of information before it can print up that simple message: 'You have left the bathroom light on' for you. That may be why it takes its time.

There is learning at work here too. For the fact that you have left the bathroom light on two or three times is fed into your computer. Before leaving the house on a future occasion your depth mind may prompt you: 'Better just check the lights again'. That is experience.

USING THE PRINCIPLE

The main characteristic, then, of the depth mind in relation to decisions is that it tends to work after the decision has been made. It is only when the suitcase is actually packed and in the back of the car that you remember you have left out your toothbrush.

In decisions involving moral values – right and wrong, good and bad – we call this reviewing of decisions after the event conscience. 'That was wrong', says the computer in the guise of conscience. Valuing often works backwards in this way, especially where the self is concerned.

This annoying characteristic of the subconscious mind is most inconvenient for the decision maker. You want your depth mind to do its work for you *before* you are irrevocably committed.

This is where the *point of no return* concept becomes significant. This is literally the position on a flight where the pilot must go on if he is in trouble rather than turn back home. By extension, it means that point in time after you have decided you cannot change your mind. This, of course, is rarely one position: there is usually a continuum of points, with the costs of changing your mind escalating as you proceed down it. For decisions soon begin to set hard, like cement. Despite that scale or continuum, it is useful to try to identify your point of no return.

By design or accident, then, decisions tend to have what could be compared to an engagement period before marriage. You have proposed and been accepted, the decision is made. You are engaged but not actually married. The decision has yet to be fully implemented. The wedding ceremony should be your point of no return – 'for better or worse, for richer or poorer, in sickness or in health'.

During that engagement period in any decision, provided you are acting in good faith, your depth mind may well say 'this isn't right for you'. You may have to distinguish that voice from the pressures of other people or the natural cold feet of anyone facing a vital decision. Do you recall the point I made earlier, namely that anxiety can distort both judgement and intuition?

Hotelman Conrad Hilton was once trying to buy an old hotel in Chicago whose owners promised to sell to the highest bidder. Several days before the deadline date for sealed bids Hilton submitted a hastily made 165,000 dollar offer. He went to bed that night feeling vaguely disturbed and woke next morning with a hunch that his bid was not high enough. 'That didn't feel right to me', he later wrote. 'Another figure kept coming, 180,000 dollars. It satisfied me. It seemed fair. It felt right. I changed my bid to the larger figure on that hunch. When they were opened the closest bid to mine was 179,000 dollars.'

Can you think of a similar incident in your career so far?

Hilton was fortunate in that he still had time to change his decision. Nor was he hooked on the notion that once you have made a decision it shows want of character to change your mind. It may do *after* your point of no return, but not *before* it. 'A wise man changes his mind, a fool never.'

It has been discovered that any decision will prod the depth mind into action. You flip a coin between a holiday in France and one in Spain. 'Heads it's France', you conclude firmly. A few hours later you know beyond a shred of doubt that you really want to go to Spain. As long as you haven't booked your tickets irrevocably, change your mind!

By making a conscious effort to review experience you can develop your depth mind into a formidable instrument. Trusting it is important. You should also develop a special kind of inward sensitivity, so that you can pick up the delicate signals, that thought which stirs imperceptibly, like a leaf touched by the air, telling you that something is moving. As Conrad Hilton writes: 'I know when I have a problem and have done all I can to figure it, I keep listening in a sort of inside silence until something clicks and I feel a right answer.'

For the best descriptions of the depth mind at work in business decisions we turn again to Lord Thomson. In his autobiography *After I was Sixty* (Hamish Hamilton, 1975), he mused on the impulses and skills that led him to success-fully pursue his distinguished career long after most of us have retired:

> I must now ask myself: what was it that gave me this self-confidence, this determination and adventurous spirit in business . . . at 67?
>
> It was at least partly due to my discovery over a fairly long period, but more than ever during these latter years in Edinburgh and London, that experience was a very important element in the management side of business and it was, of course, the one thing that I had plenty of. I could go further and say that for management to be good it generally must be experienced. To be good at anything at all requires a lot of practice, and to be really good at taking decisions you have to have plenty of practice at taking decisions. The more one is exposed to the necessity of making decisions, the better one's decision making becomes.

At various times during my business life I have had to take some important decisions and, particularly in the early days, I often got these wrong. But I found later that the early mistakes and, for that matter, the early correct decisions stood me in good stead. Most of the problems that I was confronted with in London were in one way or another related to those earlier ones. It was often a matter of just adding some zeros to figures and the sums were the same. In a great many instances I knew the answer immediately.

I cannot explain this scientifically, but I was entirely convinced that, through the years, in my brain as in a computer, I had stored details of the problems themselves, the decisions reached and the results obtained; everything was neatly filed away there for future use. Then, later, when a new problem arose, I would think it over and, if the answer was not immediately apparent, I would let it go for a while, and it was as if it went the rounds of the brain cells looking for guidance that could be retrieved, for by next morning, when I examined the problem again, more often than not the solution came up right away. That judgement seemed to be come to almost unconsciously, and my conviction is that during the time I was not consciously considering the problem, my subconscious had been turning it over and relating it to my memory; it had been held up to the light of the experiences I had had in past years, and the way through the difficulties became obvious. I am pretty sure other older men have had this same evidence of the brain's subconscious work.

This makes it all very easy, you may say. But, of course, it doesn't happen easily. That bank of experience from which I was able to draw in the later years was not easily funded.

The International Business Machines Company – one

of the world's great business organizations – have had for many years a single word as their motto. A sign over every executive's desk spells it out: 'Think'. Let us be honest with ourselves and consider how averse we all are to doing just that. Thinking is work. In the early stages of a man's career it is very hard work. When a difficult decision or problem arises, how easy it is, after looking at it superficially, to give up thinking about it. It is easy to put it from one's mind. It is easy to decide that it is insoluble, or that something will turn up to help us. Slopping and inconclusive thinking becomes a habit. The more one does it the more one is unfitted to think a problem through to a proper conclusion.

If I have any advice to pass on, as a successful man, it is this: if one wants to be successful, one must think; one must think until it hurts. One must worry a problem in one's mind until it seems there cannot be another aspect of it that hasn't been considered. Believe me, that is hard work and, from my close observation, I can say that there are few people indeed who are prepared to perform this arduous and tiring work. But let me go further and assure you of this: while, in the early stages, it is hard work and one must accept it as such, later one will find that it is not so difficult, the thinking apparatus has become trained; it is trained even to do some of the thinking subconsciously as I have shown. The pressure that one had to use on one's poor brain in the early stages no longer is necessary; the hard grind is rarely needed; one's mental computer arrives at decisions instantly or during a period when the brain seems to be resting. It is only the rare and most complex problems that require the hard toil of protracted mental effort.

By chance I happened to be reading Eugen Herrigel's *Zen in the Art of Archery* (Vintage Books, 1999) at the same time as

Thomson's book. It is an account by a young German philosopher, the first European to go to Japan in order to understand Zen. To that end he studied archery under a great master named Kenzo Awa for over five years, practising endlessly the various techniques of drawing the bow. But he learnt that to master an art, technical knowledge is not enough. Technique has to be transcended; the art has to grow naturally out of the unconscious. Zen is clearly holistic; it places much emphasis on the depth mind. As conscious analysis and calculation recede, the archer allows his depth mind to think and decide for him. The shot 'falls' from the bow like a ripe fruit from the bough. Thomson is really saying much the same about business decision making. Both the master archer and the master businessman make it look simple, but years of thought and practice lie behind their easy skills.

SUMMARY

For a long time we have known that the unconscious mind plays a strategic role in creative thinking, but the part it plays in the decisions of experienced managers is new territory that I have opened up in this book. You should have picked up the following points from Lord Thomson's advice for more reflection and action:

- *The way to become good at decision making is to make lots of decisions in your field*
  Practice makes perfect. That proverb will apply to decision making if practice is based upon sound principles.
- *See the relationships between your decisions, despite differences of time, place and scale*

Thomson saw connections between the problems he faced in Canada and those he encountered in London. Those earlier decisions, correct and incorrect, were in the computer: 'In a great many instances I knew the answer immediately'.

- *Look on your brain as a mental computer*
  Earlier sequences of decisions and results are fed into the mind. Where solutions are not easily apparent, allow time for your depth mind to work on it. As a principle, a period of close enquiry and reflection should be followed either by a change of subject or a period of inactivity.
- *Shun mental laziness*
  At all stages of your career conscious thinking demands some very hard work. You have to be prepared for that effort. If you do it when young you will reap the benefit of an exceptionally good depth mind.
- *Few people are willing to make the effort*
  That is a challenging comment. It could be good news for you. As the proverb says, 'The many fail, the one succeeds'.

KEY POINTS: YOUR DEPTH MIND

- The functions of the conscious mind – analysing, synthesizing and valuing – can also take place on a deeper level. Your depth mind can dissect for you, just as your stomach juices can break down food into its elements.
- The depth mind, for example, is capable of analysing data that you may not have known you had taken in, and comparing it with what is filed away in your memory bank.
- The depth mind is capable of more than analysis. It is also

close to the seat of your memory and the repository of your values. It is also a workshop where creative synthesis can be made by an invisible workmanship.

- An organic analogy for its function is the womb, where after conception a baby is formed and grows from living matter.
- You may also have experienced the value of thinking of the depth mind's neighbour we call conscience in the form of guilt feelings or even remorse. Conscience is useful because its red light may tell you that your decision making has led to a wrong move.

> *Dust as we are, the immortal spirit grows*
> *Like harmony in music; there is a dark*
> *Inscrutable workmanship that reconciles*
> *Discordant elements, makes them cling together*
> *In one society.*
>
> William Wordsworth

9

OPTIONS

'When your enemy has only two options open to him you can be sure that he will choose the third.'

Bismarck

In this chapter you will read about the second important aspect of decision making or problem solving. Having established the truth to the best of your ability, you are then in a position to generate and choose between possible courses of action or solutions, here called *options*. By the end of it you should have a clear idea of the structure of options and know how to manage the process of selecting from them the best one for your purpose.

It was 17 September 1862. Cannon thundered along the battle lines as two armies of Blue and Grey soldiers faced each other across the Antietam Creek. Then General Ambrose Burnside gave order to advance. The Union army was to storm across the creek and attack the enemy at close quarters. The route he chose to send them led over the narrow bridge across the creek, the only one in the vicinity. The Confederate gunners in the batteries specially placed to command the bridge could hardly believe their eyes. They swept away regiment after regiment with grapeshot. The slaughter was appalling.

General Burnside had failed to discover that the Antietam Creek in this region was only about 3 feet deep. It could have been forded by infantry or cavalry at any point with perfect safety. Of the battle at Antietam and the general who lost it for him President Lincoln said somewhat bitterly: 'Only he could have wrung so spectacular a defeat from the jaws of victory.'

Burnside had acted on the assumption that he had only one option open to him. In fact we now know that he was wrong. He had not carried out a thorough reconnaissance. His decision rested upon an erroneous understanding of his situation.

In the same way, business histories are full of disasters that came about because all the options were not considered. 'We cannot put the price up', 'We cannot risk a strike,' 'We cannot possibly afford a 5 per cent increase in wages' are all examples of refusal to consider a particularly unpleasant option. It may, however, not even be an unpleasant option that is ignored; 'I never thought of *that*' is an all too common cry.

Considering options is inseparable from gathering information about the situation. As you can scan a situation, analysing and sifting it, you will see the more obvious possibilities for action. In the second phase of thinking, when you have grasped the essentials of the problem or situation, you switch your mental forces to a new front: reviewing and perhaps adding to that list of possibilities.

DEVELOPING A RANGE OF OPTIONS

It is important in this phase to understand what you are seeking. You are not seeking all the possibilities of action. That step, so often recommended in management textbooks, is a recipe for indecision. Take chess. You might assume that a computer can look at every possible move in the game. That is not so. A very ordinary game will run to twenty-five moves, and if a computer wants to consider every possibility equally, it has to consider one thousand million, million, million, etc. (1 followed by 75 zeros) combinations of moves.

Suppose computers could consider a million moves a second, it would take many millions of times longer than the entire history of our planetary system for them to sort out all the possibilities. Therefore a computer, like you or me, looks only a few moves ahead. The computer's weakness here lies in its absence of a valuing faculty. The chess master knows at once which moves are feasible, and that means worth considering.

The word *feasible* is crucially important because it saves you time. When it comes to scanning options it helps immeasurably if you know what you are looking for. *Possible* is a much wider term embracing everything that could be done within the limits of the situation, whereas *feasible* narrows it down a little to what can be done with existing resources.

You may remember that logicians analyse syllogisms by reducing them to a skeleton and lettering the parts, so that their relationships can be seen more clearly. I shall use much the same principle here.

The first thing to do is to sort out the feasible options from the greater number of possible options. Imagine yourself as a coin dealer or a diamond merchant sifting quickly through someone's collection and choosing the five or six specimens that are worth considering for purchase.

Then you need to proceed by *elimination*. So the process resembles a cone, as shown in The Process of Elimination below.

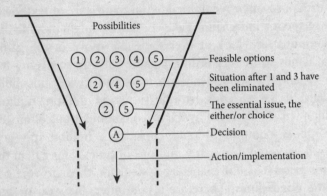

The process of elimination

It is common sense, as well as scientific orthodoxy now, that it is easier to disprove things than to prove them. Theoretically you cannot prove anything finally and conclusively, but for practical purposes you can, in so far as your approximation to truth is near enough for everyday needs. Science is constantly trying to devise tests to support or disprove hypotheses. All that a truthful scientist can say about a hypothesis is that it has survived all those tests up to this date.

As Einstein replied to a lady who was congratulating him on news of an astronomical observation that seemed to prove his theory of relativity: 'Madam, a thousand experiments cannot ever prove me right; a single experiment can prove me wrong.'

Your aim in working on the feasible options is to reduce them to two alternatives – either this or that – as soon as possible. But remember the proverb 'More haste, less speed'.

Alternatives, in the strict sense, are mutually exclusive. To marry either Mary or Jane is an alternative: in our society you cannot marry both. The first thing to do is to check if the alternatives are truly alternative. After all, they may not have survived the mental obstacle course you have created for them unless you liked them both. If, in fact, they are not attractive – if they are the two 'least worst' options – you may be pleased to drop one of them. But these are situations when you can opt for both of them, possibly in sequence – the 'trial-and-error' method. Or you can combine, mix or blend them in some other way.

The do-nothing option is sometimes worth considering

If neither alternative attracts you, and you cannot produce a satisfactory compromise, it is always worth asking yourself, Do I have to take action at all? The option of doing nothing, of deciding not to act, is always worth considering. Sometimes the proposed cure promises to be worse than the disease, but the decision to do nothing must be taken for a very good reason and not because you cannot think of another way.

As a variation, if there is no obvious winner, nor a trade-off between objective achievement and implementability, you may want to choose the option that is most likely to keep your options open. The strategy of keeping options open for as long as possible has much to commend it.

Option check-list

Constantly ask yourself and your colleagues these questions:

- Which possibilities are feasible, given our limitations?
- Which of the feasible options are the true alternatives?

- Are they mutually exclusive, or can we do
  - (a) Both or
  - (b) Some creative combination of the two?
- Will the resulting compromise achieve our objective better than either of the discrete courses?
- Would it be better to do nothing?
- In what circumstances should we abandon the policy of keeping our options open for as long as possible?

You may object that there often is not time to work steadily through the cone. But even in the most tense situations it is best to keep your head and mentally check out the most likely possibilities.

EXERCISE 8: An option problem

You are the engineer on flight BA 507 en route from London to Caracas. At 30,000 feet all four engines stop for no apparent reason. What do you do?

(a) Guess the cause and work on that
(b) Work through the standard checklist

You choose (b). Having completed the checklist you still have not found the cause of engine failure. You are now at 8,000 feet. What do you do next? Send out distress signals? Fix parachutes?

(You have one minute from now to answer this question. Turn to p. 181 for the answer when you have jotted yours down.)

Intuitive thinkers tend to jump to the either-or situation without apparently going through a conscious process of eliminating alternatives. Albert Speer, one of Hitler's intimates, noted this tendency. His close associates even joked openly about it to Hitler's face, without him taking offence. Thus his standard phrase, 'There are two possibilities', would be used by one of his secretaries, in his presence, often in the most everyday context. She would say: 'There are two possibilities. Either it is going to rain or it is not going to rain.'

Hitler's failure to think systematically about military situations, compounded by a growing distrust of those generals and staff officers around him who could, plus the effects of stress upon his undoubted natural flair as a commander, lost him the Second World War.

FALSE ASSUMPTIONS:
SOME EXAMPLES FROM HISTORY

Once you have acquired some knowledge about the apparent limits or limitations in a problem or situation, you should test them for reality. This is value thinking: are they real or true limits, or are they false ones? Finding out may require some physical work. Had he carried out a proper reconnaissance, General Burnside would have discovered that Antietam Creek was not a real limitation to the movement of soldiers. Far from being a boundary, it was an open gateway.

Military history abounds with examples of generals exploiting the infinite capacity of the human mind to make false assumptions about limits. Before his invasion of Italy early in his career Napoleon read the works of many writers who repeated that it was impracticable to consider crossing the Alps in winter with a large army. His staff officers agreed. But Napoleon always thought for himself, and he challenged that view:

The winter is not the most unfavourable season for the passage of lofty mountains. The snow is then firm, the weather settled, and there is nothing to fear from

avalanches, the real and only danger to be apprehended in
the Alps. On those high mountains, there are often very
fine days in December, of a dry cold, with extreme calmness in the air.

Hitler made a similar decision in 1940, when he brushed
aside the received conclusion of the German General Staff
that it would be impossible to take armoured divisions
through the wooded hills of the Ardennes – and was proved
to be right.

In the 1930s the British Imperial General Staff spent much
time resolving how to defend Britain's colonies in the Far
East. They fortified the island of Singapore as a bastion,
constructing powerful batteries of heavy guns to make it
impregnable from the sea and a great naval base to shelter the
fleet that would be sent there in war time. Little time was
spent on the possibility that Singapore would be attacked by
land across the causeway that joined it to the mainland. The
British military planners assumed that the mountainous jungle
of Malaya was impassable to a modern army. Nor did they
spend much money on air defences, for the admirals were
convinced that aircraft could not pose much threat to
warships.

In 1941 the plan was put into action. Two battleships, the
Prince of Wales and the *Repulse* were despatched to the Far
East to overawe the Japanese. To the surprise of the British
generals, however, the Japanese did not obligingly land in
front of the British guns but in the north on the mainland.
The two British battleships sailed to intercept the invasion
fleet but were both sunk by Japanese aircraft. The Japanese
struck south through the jungle with ease, and attacked
Singapore from the landward side. As the large guns were
all pointing the wrong way the city fell within days and

10,000 British and Australian soldiers became prisoners. In Churchill's words it was 'the largest capitulation in British history'.

Again, the business world is full of companies that made false assumptions about limits. The Japanese 'invasion' of the British motorcycle industry provides an example: the British motorcycle firms assumed that the only competition was amongst themselves.

SOME LIMITATIONS AFFECTING MANAGEMENT CHOICES

Knowing where to look for limitations will save time. Here are four suggested key areas where care should be taken to establish the real limits in a given situation.

Time

Perhaps the first question you should ask in any decision making situation is, 'How much time have we got?' Is that the real amount of time? Why is it not more – or less? Test the limit, especially if someone else is laying down a time scale for you. They may be making a false assumption about how much time is available. Many problems can be solved if we adopt a longer time scale for their solution. But that requires patience – a management quality that is often in short supply.

Information

No decision maker ever has all the information he or she needs. Again, there has to be a judgement at some point. For the quest for information is subject to the law of diminishing returns. At first you gain a great deal of information in a short space of time; gradually you are spending more-and-more time and effort to acquire what is in effect less-and-less relevant information. The real limit is the point in a given situation where you judge that the cost in time and money of obtaining more information becomes too high.

Resources

There will be a variety of resources, but the obvious ones for a businessman include the amount of money you have available. Remember the 'opportunity cost': if you use your resources for this purpose you will be detracting from your resources elsewhere; in other words, you will make a limitation for yourself in another sector. Machinery is another resource. It is no good promising a customer 1,000 items a week at once if your machines can only produce half that number.

Knowledge

In any study of successes and failures in business diversification one factor stands out: the knowledge of managers. This embraces both knowledge of the business field in question and knowledge of management – including leadership, decision making and communication. If your managers are limited in experience and in quality, then that sets a limit on what you can attempt.

GENERATING MORE OPTIONS

Decision implies real choice. The more feasible options within the broad constraints of time and space you have to choose from the better your decision is likely to be.

Even if there appears to be one course open once the truth has been established, an experienced manager will cast around in his mind to see if there is not another option. By closing thought down too early, the good option can become the enemy of the best option.

Here imaginative thinking comes into its own. We must draw a sharp distinction between *unconscious* assumptions (which may, of course, be true or untrue) and the *conscious* assumptions or suppositions that we can use as a portable step ladder in imaginative thinking:

Supposing we had an extra million pounds, what would we do then?

Let us *assume* that the trade union will not object to this plan, how would we implement it?

Assuming, for the moment, that the Board agrees . . .

Imagination can sometimes be employed to construct assumptions in order to test others.

Looking back on that abortive invasion of Cuba – the Bay of Pigs fiasco – mentioned in a previous chapter the then Secretary of State, Dean Rusk, recalled that President Kennedy had conceived a totally unrealistic idea of what a puny brigade of Cuban exiles could possibly achieve. 'I should have told the President', said Rusk, 'that we might want to do it with American forces. 'Ask your military chiefs of staff', I should have said to him, 'to assume that American troops would be used. Then get them to tell you what they must have before they invaded Cuba – what air support, ground divisions and naval back-up. If we had made that assumption we should never have made such an error.'

Creative imagination comes more into play, however, when you are thinking about how to use existing resources. Your mind can easily become dominated by what some psychologists have called *functional fixedness*, the tendency to see things in association with a given function. The conventional mind accepts these sorts of assumptions: a hammer is for hammering in nails, an army camp is for housing soldiers – if there are no more soldiers, knock it down. Children, before they acquire functional fixedness, are much more imaginative in their play. An object for them can take on any number of uses. The way holiday camps came into being provides an excellent example of creative imagination at work:

> Billy Butlin was a circus man. When he looked over disused army camps in 1946 he conceived the idea of using them as holiday camps. He even kept the army's tannoy system he found in the camps. He was told it wouldn't work, but Butlin's Holiday Camps played a major part in meeting the needs of the British people, especially before the era of cheap overseas holiday packages.

In imaginative thinking intended to overcome functional fixedness it is useful to remember the principle of artificially restraining or disciplining the critical, analytical, reasoning function. Make the analysers wait their turn. Let your mind off its habitual leashes so that it roams freely wherever it wills to go in the field you have chosen.

When it comes to trying to think about fresh possibilities, there are two kinds of people. The first, when confronted with a new idea, will react in a distinctly negative way. By clear, logical thinking they may soon be able to show that the idea is wrong or that the plan is unworkable. The second type will react differently. They will toy with it, and speculate what the implications might be if the idea could be put into practice. Because of the novelty of the proposal their impulse is to wish it could be shown to be true.

A condition of creativity seems to be a readiness to side with, empathize with and explore the possibilities of fresh ideas. It also seems to be compatible with the attitude of discriminating criticism previously discussed. The attitude consists, in fact, of vigorous attention to ideas which, because they important, merit criticism in the interests of their refinement or extension.

The principle of *suspending judgement*, as it is called, lies at the heart of the popular technique of brainstorming. Here the evaluation of ideas is deliberately kept at bay until a sufficient number have been produced by the free-wheeling processes of thought. But the barrier erected by premature criticism in creative thinking was recognized long before 1927, the year Alex Osborn invented brainstorming. Johann Schiller, the celebrated German poet who trained as a lawyer, then became a military surgeon and ended his career as professor of history at Jena in 1788, once wrote to a friend:

The reason for your complaint (about not being creative) lies, it seems to me, in the constraint which your intellect imposes upon your imagination. Here I will make an observation, and illustrate it by an allegory. Apparently, it is not good – and indeed it hinders the creative work of the mind – if the intellect examines too closely the ideas already pouring in, as it were, at the gates. Hence your complaints of unfruitfulness, for you reject too soon and discriminate too severely.

Although either may be premature, it is always useful to bear in mind the distinction between negative and constructive criticism. The negative critic is like an underwater fisherman equipped with a gun and various darts – killer phrases that he launches at any fish he sees stirring in your depth mind, such as:

- We tried that before
- Let's get back to reality
- I don't like the idea
- Good idea in theory – but impracticable
- You'll make us a laughing stock
- Where did you dig that one up from?
- It's never been tried before
- It won't work here
- It can't be done
- We've always done it this way
- Costs too much

A true critic might be defined as one who expresses a reasoned opinion on any matter involving a judgement of its value, such as truth, beauty or technical quality. He appreciates what value is there. The constructive part comes into play when such a critic suggests ways in which value can be added to the idea or matter under scrutiny.

ASSESSING THE CONSEQUENCES

The game of consequences lies at the heart of the rational approach to decision making. But consequences, when you examine them carefully, are not susceptible to precise calculation.

As a principle, the more familiar a situation is to you the more you will be able to judge its consequences. Alternatively, someone else's experience may give you clues, which is why history is so important. The newer the situation, as a corollary, the less likely you are to be able to predict consequences.

Now all situations are partly old or familiar (at least to someone else if not to you), and partly unique. History both does and does not repeat itself. You can see how difficult it then becomes to predict outcomes.

In 1965 the Americans decided to mount a strategic bombing offensive against the North Vietnamese forces. So they had to build airbases near Saigon in the south. To protect these bases they sent 3,000 marines. But the US Marine Corps is trained to be aggressive. Rather than sit around their perimeters the commanders on the ground decided on a policy of active defence and defined their objective in terms of killing the Vietcong. Soon more soldiers had to be transported there to support them. And more. And more.

Slipshod thinking of this kind about consequences is all too common. After such events the argument becomes a matter of historical judgement: could the Americans have foreseen such results and also, ought they to have done so? These are questions of responsibility and blame, involving our powers to make some often very fine distinctions between reasons and excuses. It is better to think thoroughly about possible and probable consequences in advance: the more that can be identified the better.

THE IMPORTANCE OF PROBABILITY

There is a danger that the more your mind unravels possible consequences the less likely you are to do anything. Fortunately for us, we cannot foresee all the obvious and hidden consequences of all the options open to us at any one time: we have to take some sort of a risk. In business decisions it is usually the case that the larger the risk the greater is the potential gain. That principle is always worth bearing in mind. Risk taking seems to be inseparable from decision making. So what are the guidelines?

The chief principle is that risks should be taken only after being carefully calculated. This means you will have to make a very thorough effort, using your imagination as well as all the relevant methods of quantification, to calculate as precisely as possible the nature and degree of the risks involved. Then you will be in a position to see what can be done to minimize the risks by prudent foresight and contingency planning. Paul Getty once said: 'When I go into any business deal my chief thoughts are on how I'm going to save myself if things go wrong.'

The proposed benefits should warrant the risk. A successful investment banker, for example, will ensure that on his ventures of capital, the upside potential for him is far in excess of the downside risk. If he gets it right on any given proposition, his investment and bank will make many times its original stake. Even if an investment is a complete failure, as long as he or she has exercised proper care, the bank should still lose no more than the money it invested. The critical factor is always to get the odds right on each investment and only to invest when the upside potential is high in relation to the initial sum advanced.

Knowing that you can accept the precisely predicted

consequences of failure is a sign that you have properly explored the risk element of a decision. Ask yourself, What is the worst possible outcome? Am I prepared to accept it if necessary? Both asking and answering those two questions will greatly ease the task of making a difficult decision.

The various systematic ways of exploring the outcomes of alternative courses of action, using diagrams and mathematical calculations of the odds, are taught in business schools. But I doubt if more than one in ten managers ever makes use of them in work situations. Yet the principle of exploring probabilities as far as possible is sound. These days exploring the probabilities of each outcome can often be greatly aided by computers. But computers can never make up your mind. Remember, you are always dealing with estimated probabilities. Therefore results will depend on how good you are at that form of judgement. Even where genuine doubts about estimates exist, however, it is at least useful to be able to examine them as thoroughly as possible.

SUMMARY

At the core of making decisions lies the activity of collecting, assessing and choosing from a set of options. If there is genuinely only one course of action open, there is hardly a decision to be made. The options considered should be feasible. It is useful to aim to reduce the list systematically by a process of elimination until you are left with the two alternatives. The more relevant information you can gather both before and during this process, the easier it will be.

When considering options the chief enemy of effective decision making is entertaining false assumptions about either your own limitations or those of your competitors. You have to be objective about what you have at your disposal: time, knowledge, resources and knowledge. Always be ruthless about the true facts of the case.

This thinking – partly analytical, partly valuing – should give way to creative thinking if it is felt necessary to generate some new options. Here you and your colleagues need to be able to suspend judgement, so that the dogs of criticism do not tear every new born idea to shreds.

Even the most original idea or course of action, however, will have predictable consequences that have to be explored as objectively as possible. Indeed, the rational way to make decisions is to assess options by weighing their outcomes, both in the short term and in the longer term perspective. Desired outcomes are so because they realize the purpose, aims and objectives of the organization.

Risk is a dimension in many decisions, not least in business life. Risks have to be carefully calculated. Computers can aid managers in a growing number of instances but they should still be seen as auxiliaries to human judgement. When considering the benefits of a risk, attention must be given to the consequences of incurring the loss or danger that is at the heart of the risk. Commitment control – or the ability and willingness to say no – is vital. The assessment of probability can give you guidance what to do. As Cicero said, 'Probabilities guide the decisions of wise men.'

KEY POINTS: OPTIONS

- Notice the word *options* rather than *alternatives*. An alternative is literally one of two courses open. Decision makers who lack skill tend to jump far too quickly to the either-or alternatives. They do not give enough time and mental energy to generating at least three or four possibilities.

- You need to open your mind into wide focus to consider all possibilities, and that is where creative thinking comes in. But then your valuing faculty must come into play to identify the feasible options – the ones that may or can be done, the practicable ones.

- When considering your options remember that it tends to be easier to discard an option rather than to choose it. In other words, we are often better at knowing what we don't want to do rather than what we do want to do.

- While considering options you should constantly ask yourself whether or not you are overlooking some feasible course of action, perhaps because it is just too obvious.

- Always check your assumptions. The less hidden they are, the better.

- As a general principle, if you accumulate enough information you may not need to make a conscious decision. For the decision will, as it were, be made for you. If there is no other feasible alternative it is comparatively easy to make up your mind what to do.

Guests sleep well in the Inn of Decision.
Arab proverb

10

ARGUING

'The faintest of all human passions
is the love of Truth'
A. E. Houseman

'Gentlemen, I take it we are all in complete agreement on the decision here.' Alfred P. Sloan, the head of General Motors, looked around the committee room table. His senior managers nodded in assent. 'Then', continued Sloan, 'I propose we postpone further discussion of this matter until our next meeting to give ourselves time to develop disagreement and perhaps gain some understanding of what the decision is about.'

Several centuries earlier, Shakespeare had expressed the same truth in a sentence: 'Rightly to be great is not to stir without great argument'. By 'great argument' Shakespeare meant a debate of high quality upon the reasons for and against the various courses of action. That is just what Sloan had sensed was lacking in his committee.

Personal ways of thinking it out with others vary considerably. Some leaders favour an argumentative style.

Margaret Thatcher, like Winston Churchill, was an intuitive leader with a strong personality, someone who thought for herself and came to some firm conclusions. Strength in this case means tenacity of perseverance. Such a person is not easily dislodged from an opinion, and perhaps never so from a conviction. He of she may not appear to be a good listener, but such leaders are persuadable. Paradoxically, some leaders who seem to be 'good listeners', those who nod and smile at you and appear to be intent upon your words, are not in fact persuadable: they are acting a part.

If you want to dislodge the Churchill or Thatcher type of thinker, therefore, you must be prepared to stand your ground and argue. You may even have to shout. Whatever your voice level, your reasons must be extra-strong or compelling to move your leader from a partly dug-in entrenched position. But, because intuitive thinkers rely so much on their depth minds, a reserve on the day does not necessarily spell defeat. Your arguments may appear to be trounced in the heated and noisy argument, but a few days later the penny may drop as the depth mind of the other person does its work.

Argumentative thinking in organizations is not the only, or necessarily the best, style. It has its drawbacks. The war of attrition between the trench lines of opinion can be very wearing on subordinates or colleagues. In the heat and dust of conflict things can be said which were better left unsaid. It calls for a high degree of trust and strong, persuasive team members.

On the other hand, argument gets the adrenalin flowing; it stimulates the mind in a way that the cool, detached reasoning advocated by management textbooks does not. It makes the team member or colleague work much harder at presenting his or her counsel on what should be done.

Between the poles of hot, noisy argument and an academic discourse there are many positions for you to choose from. Nor should you rigidly adhere to one point on that scale. In some instances you may want to contend and disagree based upon a firm (if ultimately moveable) point of view; in others you may want to generate an atmosphere of discussion rather than argument, where each possibility is considered by presenting the considerations for and against without prior commitment upon your part or anyone else's. It depends partly on the situation, partly on the matter under consideration, and partly upon your temperament.

Check your own thinking style

- Would you describe yourself as an argumentative thinker, one who likes to reason with others in a way that proceeds by argument?
- Or is your normal style more like that of the discussion leader, preferring a situation where neither party has already taken up a fixed position?
- Can you adapt your own approach in a flexible way to the style of others?

Whatever approach you adopt – or have thrust upon you – you should constantly remember the ultimate aim of argument. It is not to win or to avoid losing (that is another drawback of the conflict model of reasoning; it encourages this competitive mentality which often goes with being a high achiever).

The aim of argument is the truth, or at least greater clarity about the issue at stake or the true alternatives. The very word comes from the Latin *arguere*, to make clear. It should be essentially a rational process, a sifting of the consequences of a proposed course of action, or of several courses of action, so that the balance sheet of arguments for and against can be plainly read by the experienced and unprejudiced eye.

What is impermissible is that there should be no discussion, debate or argument in organizational life. For there will always be matters about which reasonable men and women may reasonably disagree. It is the ends and quality of the debate, more than the personal styles of those involved, that matter most.

Argument of the best quality is usually conducted by rational men and women who wish to become clear about what they should or do believe. They may be partly clear but not wholly so, or they may not be completely convinced. They want to hear other points of view. They are in principle willing to change and accept those other points of view if they are more coherent and supported by the weight of evidence. They will entertain any opinion or adopt any of the proposed courses of action as long as reason – the balance of consequences judged in the light of the common purpose – emerges from the argument to favour it.

We owe this concept of argument to the Greeks. Thucydides put into the mouth of the most famous Athenian statesman Pericles these words:

> The great impediment of action is in our opinion not discussion but the want of that knowledge which is gained by discussion prior to action. For we have a peculiar power of thinking before we act too, whereas other men are courageous from ignorance but hesitate upon reflection.

In the tradition of that Athenian Golden Age, John Milton gave eloquent expression to argument as the God-given method by which rational men reached a consensus about the truth. In a pamphlet written during the English Civil War protesting against Parliament's imposition of censorship, he wrote:

> Where there is much to learn, there of necessity will be much arguing, much writing, many opinions; for opinion

in good men is but knowledge in the making . . . Give me
the liberty to know, to utter and to argue freely according
to conscience, above all liberties.

Milton, of course, was convinced that truth existed objectively and that we tend to doubt the strength of the truth to
prevail. 'Let her and Falsehood grapple; who ever knew
Truth put to the worse in a free and open encounter?'

HOW TO GET IT WRONG

Rational argument, a 'free and open encounter', implies
some rules, some common acceptance of criteria and a
common commitment to truth. These will reduce the possibilities of errors, fallacies or deliberate cheating. If you
encourage the winning-at-all-costs mentality, incidentally,
you must expect more deliberate foul play. Tricks and
cheating involve such motives, but you should also be on the
alert for slipshod thinking as well. The following list of
professional fouls, fallacies, slipshod thinking and pitfalls
into which the unwary step, is far from exhaustive. But it
gives you some idea what to look for.

1 Playing the man, not the ball

Argumentum ad hominem, as the Roman rhetoricians called
it, is argument calculated to appeal to the individual being
addressed rather than to impartial reason. One dishonest
version of it is to deliberately anger or frighten the person
you are talking to so that emotion will cloud their thinking
processes. You often see boxers trying to 'psych' each other
in this way before a contest. A deliberately offensive or
insolent manner, or making fun of matters the other person

obviously feels deeply about can serve to unbalance them. Once you understand the trick, the remedy is obvious. However annoying the other person is, you will best persuade them by keeping your temper under control.

There are plenty of other more subtle variations of arguing by concentrating on the human emotions and human frailties of your opponent. They are given below, along with their original Latin names:

Argumentum ad crumenam	An argument to the purse – that is, one touching the hearer's pocket.
Argumentum ad ignorantiam	An argument to ignorance, that is, one depending for its effect on the hearer's not knowing something essential.
Argumentum ad invidiam	An argument to envy or prejudice, that is, appealing to those particular emotions.

Almost any appeals to emotion, such as using words with an emotional bias – 'bloody obstinate' rather than 'stubborn' or 'firm' – come under this heading.

2 Argument by analogy

This need not be a dishonest trick, more a potential pitfall. Analogy in the form of metaphor or simile is useful for the purposes of understanding an unfamiliar topic (see Chapter 11) and as a guide to further investigation. But its reliability must be constantly tested. For example, it may be used to *suggest* a conclusion, but is incapable of *establishing* one.

Analogy is often linked to inference, which is based on the presumption that things that are known to be alike in certain respects will also be found to be alike in other respects, even though knowledge about some of these may be limited. An example of this might be that a product, because its development in some respects resembles that of a person, must with the passing of time, grow feeble and die.

Analogy rests on similarities, then, between related or apparently unrelated phenomena. But looking at those points of similarity can blind you to the divergences or differences. If pressed too far, analogy always breaks down. Therefore the best way to deal with it is by examining the alleged analogy in detail and pointing out where and why it breaks down.

Variations on the theme of arguing by analogy include 'Everyone is in the same boat' and 'Everyone is doing it'. Both imply analogies with other nations, societies, organizations or generalized individuals. The argument for pilfering, for example, tends to be that everyone is pilfering.

These analogies always break down if examined in detail. Take national unemployment, for example. Other nations may be in the same boat, for the same broad reasons, but under the microscope the ways in which their boat is different, or their management is different, or the national characteristics and situation is different, is conveniently left out.

The argument that everyone is doing it is usually a demonstrably false assumption. Moreover, numbers do not count in moral arguments. Therefore social surveys are of little value here. Arguments of this kind, anyway, usually fall under the heading of excuses rather than proper reasons.

3 Rationalizing

Excuses or reasons? That question leads us to rationalizing, or giving respectable reasons for actions. Hypocrisy, it has been said, is a tribute that vice pays to virtue. On the same principle, rationalization is the tribute our irrational selves pay to reason.

Rationalizing can be a legitimate activity. You may have made a decision on intuitive grounds, and then seek to make it conform to rational principles.

In the pejorative sense, to rationalize means to attribute something, for example one's own actions, to rational and creditable motives without analysing the true (especially subconscious) motives. Giving excuses is an example of principle, because excuses are plausible but untrue reasons for conduct.

It is obviously very difficult when you are dealing with yourself, let alone other people, to discern between reasons and rationalizations. One strategy to adopt is not to give reasons where reasons are not called for. You do not have to justify loving someone, for instance, by giving reasons. The heart has its reasons as well as the head. 'When we ask for reasons when we should not, we rationalize.'

John Henry Newman, who said this, also added a significant thought for managers to consider: 'All men have a reason, but not all men can give a reason.' In argument the clever, articulate person always has an advantage. But a wise person will sense when he is talking to someone who has a reason that he has difficulty in putting into words.

Usually negotiation of any kind is accompanied by an exchange of reasons mixed with rationalizations. Experienced managers, like judges in law courts, can sort out the reason-making from the reason-giving. Provided, of course, they are not partisans themselves.

A particularly difficult form of rationalization to detect is projection. This is where people impute (or project) their own motives or attitudes to others. A cynical or egotistical person, for example, often projects his or her own attitudes and motives to others. Even if you suspect projection, and point it out, arguments derived from amateur psychological analysis of the other person are unlikely to convince him or her. It is a useful discipline not to voice them: work on the assumption that the person you are dealing with is as rational as you are!

Perhaps the most harmful type of rationalizing is buck-passing, or projecting the blame on to someone else. This is what the bad carpenter is doing when he blames his tools. In its extreme form, it involves making scapegoats of some person or group. Ineffective managers tend to see their superiors, colleagues or team members as lacking in competence, never themselves. A common form of defence for the manager who wants to hide a deficiency in a business meeting is to call into doubt the accuracy of the figures being examined. Unless the data are obviously correct, the mere act of casting doubt deflects criticism.

4 Drawing irrelevant conclusions

The logicians call this one *ignoratio elenchi*, which means ignoring the argument or the matter at issue. You will see it done frequently in television interviews. The fallacy consists of disproving or proving something different from what is strictly in question. If, for example, the question is whether we should try to sell our goods in China, and you prove conclusively that we have failed to sell them in Japan, you are guilty of this fallacy. It is like saying 'A must be true of B', when in fact A doesn't follow from B at all. This is an example of a *non sequitur*, something that does not follow. A non sequitur always assumes an unproved cause. Thus, to say that we shall have riots this summer because youth unemployment is high is a non sequitur because it assumes rather than proves the cause. The fallacy of confusing consequence with sequence – because something happens after it, therefore it was caused by it – is a variation of the non sequitur.

Diversions, red herrings and non sequiturs come in many other shapes and sizes. Aim to become quick at detecting them. Try to see when someone is consciously or subconsciously attempting to shunt the whole discussion down a line leading to a side issue. Watch out for the assumption that once an opponent has been defeated on a trivial point, the day has somehow been won on the main matter in contention. Deal firmly with irrelevant objections (especially on points of detail), and long diversionary exercises in humour.

The remedy for all irrelevance and diversion is to state again the real question at stake.

5 Reduction to absurdity

The method of *reductio ad absurdum* is an attempt to disprove a thesis or proposed course of action by producing something that is both obviously deducible from it and obviously contrary to common sense. It can equally be used to prove a proposition by showing that its contrary involves a consequence that is similarly absurd. Thus *reductio ad absurdum* is a tactic in the vitally important game of reasoning about consequences.

If, for example, you argue that the less labour you employ the less cost you incur and that therefore to be completely cost-effective you should employ no labour at all, you are offering a *reductio ad absurdum* for the rest of the board of directors to consider. Carrying an argument to its logical conclusion nearly always produces a nonsense.

The Greek mathematician Euclid often used this method, incidentally, as a form of proof by assuming the contrary of the thing to be proved, and then showing that it led to an obvious absurdity.

6 The no decision/no action argument

'There is much to be said on both sides, so no decision can be made either way.' The more intelligent you are, the more likely you are to tumble into the pitfall of the no decision/no action argument.

As an exasperated politician once declared in the British Parliament, 'Someone should remind the Prime Minister that it is axiomatic that "the time is never quite right"; the atmosphere is always cloudy: the issue can never be sufficiently precisely defined and so it is never politic to proceed.'

Much the same kind of argument is advanced in boardrooms or in management meetings. Have you ever heard these 'arguments'?

- Leave it until we are not so busy
- We're not quite ready for that yet
- Let's hold it in abeyance
- Let's give it more thought
- Let's form a committee
- It needs more work on it
- Let's make a survey first
- A working party should look into the whole area

These responses may be genuine. 'Leave undone whatever you hesitate to do', as an Eastern sage put it, is sometimes very good advice. But these phrases may be symptoms of a manager's deep reluctance to make any decision in the face of two or more equally balanced options at a time when a decision is clearly called for.

We cannot escape the necessity for action, and the growing realization that there is much to be said on all sides does not absolve us from the need to judge where the balance of truth or wisdom lies, and then to act on that judgement. We have to choose the course of action that on the whole seems to be the best.

Closely related to the no decision/no action argument is another stock line: 'Let's not do anything about X (which admittedly needs attention), because there is another problem Y that merits our attention as well.' In skilled hands this argument can be used against doing almost anything! Because we can do nothing about starvation in central Asia, for example, let's not bother to tackle poverty in Glasgow. This dishonest argument reflects a restrictive 'either/or' type of thinking. If X and Y are both evil then both should be dealt with. Likewise, if both X and Y are good, then both should be encouraged.

The remedy for the no decision/no action argument is first to see clearly that making no decision is indeed a clear and valid option in a variety of situations.

Faced with mutually exclusive alternatives, you then have a three-way choice:

1 Alternative A
2 Alternative B
3 Opt out

If opting out is clearly an inadequate response, then you must resolve your dilemma by choosing A or B. If the choices are nearly equal it doesn't really matter which you choose, *as long as it's one of them*.

In such situations many people find it useful to flip a coin to decide. There have been reports that having flipped a coin that determines the choice, they suddenly realize that this option is not really the one they want and are thus able to select the other. As mentioned elsewhere, this is the depth mind doing its work, but late on cue. The no decision/no action argument is valid only when no action is really the best option.

7 All and some

Although arguments in the cast of formal syllogisms, with accompanying statements like 'I am being logical now', are rare in boardrooms, there are plenty of fallacious arguments put forward in the name of reason. Many of them hinge on the use of generalizations followed by deductions.

Of course some generalizations are true, and we can deduce from them. 'All men are born' is true, therefore it is equally true that if he is a man he must have been born. But most such generalizations are suspect. 'All blue collar work-ers are idle' is as untrue as 'all managers are only out for the maximum possible profit'.

As an aid to clear thinking it can be helpful to insert the phrases 'tend to be' or 'have a tendency towards'. You can get away with saying that 'women tend to be intuitive', but not with 'all women are intuitive'. It's often not very popular these days to be moderate and shun the media-catching exaggeration. But it pays off in the clarity of your thought. Caution over generalizations is not merely academic nicety. Too often decisions are based upon unwarranted statements or assumptions about what is generally the case.

Thinking revolves around the poles of the general and the particular, and getting the relationship between them as correct as possible.

Proof by selected instances is a variation of the 'all and some' fallacy. Much dishonest argument consists of selecting instances favourable to our view while conveniently ignoring other instances that are either unfavourable or downright hostile to it.

One variation of the 'all and some' argument, which causes endless domestic and professional trouble, is generalizing from selected instances *ad hominem*. Instead of saying accurately 'You have been late three times', you say 'You are *always* late'. Exaggerations intended for emphasis, signalled by such words as 'always' and 'never', rob you of truth and the psychological advantages that go with it.

Arguments using statistics are notoriously liable to 'all and some' errors. For it is often unclear whether or not generalizations can properly be drawn from the samples. If 3,986 people in Boston now prefer bran products to cornflakes for breakfast, can we infer that all Americans do? Perhaps there is a wider choice of cereals in Los Angeles.

In the first place statistics can be biased. Cooking or laundering the figures is not unknown. But more often than not is the interpretation of the figures that is biased. In order to get the best out of this important source of data you need to be able to distinguish clearly between a fact and an opinion when these are cooked together and served up on your committee room table.

8 Middle-of-the-road arguments

The assumption that the truth lies always in the mean position between two extremes is obvious nonsense. For every view can be presented as a mean between two extremes.

A second reason for distrusting this kind of argument is the fact that when you have two extreme positions and a middle one between them, the truth is just as likely to be at one end of the spectrum as in the middle. If I wanted to persuade you that two and two make five, I might point out to you that five is the safe position between the extremists who argue on the one hand that two and two make four and the other extremists who assert that two and two make six.

That is not to say, of course, that recommending a position or course on the grounds that it is a mean between two extremes is necessarily being dishonest. But it is suspect if that is your only reason for arguing its acceptance.

Another related fallacy is to use the continuity between two poles or extremes to throw in doubt a real difference between them. To take a trivial example, if a man is growing a beard it is not easy to say precisely when he has a beard or when he doesn't, but you should not imply that there is no difference between a man with a beard and one without one.

The obverse side is the common mistake in reasoning of demanding or making a sharp distinction between those with beards and those without. These are the black or white thinkers: they cannot perceive all the intermediary shades of grey that lie between them. We create a barrier to clear thinking if we try to mark off a characteristic that is not capable of being so sharply defined.

Understand 'the law of the excluded middle'. See if this is a truly either/or situation, with no middle term. If so, you are in a true dilemma. But it may be one where there is a range of possibilities between the extremes.

Here is an example of clear thinking by Edward Whymper, who, after seven unsuccessful attempts was the first person to reach the summit of the Matterhorn in July 1865.

The line which separates the difficult from the dangerous is sometimes very shadowy, but it is not an imaginary line. It is a true line without breadth. It is often easy to pass, and very hard to see. It is sometimes passed unconsciously, and the consciousness that it has been passed is felt too late. If the doubtful line is crossed consciously, deliberately, one passes from doing that which is justifiable to that which is unjustifiable.

The erroneous assumption that truth always lies in the middle of two extreme points must not be confused with true moderation. It is, of course, equally erroneous that those who take up the more extreme positions are being more 'radical' or 'honest' than their neighbours. Extremism of this kind is a strategy that pays only short-term dividends. It can be exceptionally disruptive in a negative or non-creative way. Leaders therefore tend not to be extremists. 'Moderation is a disposing, arranging, conciliatory, cementing virtue,' said Edmund Burke. 'Moderation is the virtue only of superior minds.'

SUMMARY

These suspect lines of arguments are merely examples. I have not written about the suggestive techniques of the salesman out to persuade a customer, because they are now familiar to all of us via television screens: the confident manner, the appeal to prestige, the air of authority, appeals to an undefined source, such as 'research shows ... 'experts agree', the use of pseudo-technical jargon, the uttering of some preliminary acceptable statements before the doubtful proposition, the invoking of our thought-habits, prejudices and emotions. All are evidence of the power of suggestion, the attempt to slip ideas below our guard into the safe lodging of our depth minds, where they will erupt next time we are in the supermarket. Beware of the hidden persuaders! The price of truth, like freedom, is eternal vigilance.

But bad arguments should not blind us to the merit of having great and good argument as a preliminary to decision.

The right-or-wrong, black-or-white kind of thinking should give way to a serious (but not necessarily solemn) argument about what it is reasonable or unreasonable to do in these circumstances. In many cases, it is better – if faced with a choice – to stir up a question without deciding it, than to decide it without stirring it up.

KEY POINTS: ARGUING

- To argue is to (try to) exhibit or prove something by reasoning. It comes from a Latin verb that means 'to make clear'.
- A good argument should do just that – clarify the issues at stake or the courses of action open. It is essentially an exchange of views. In it there should be reasoned presentations of views. If such argument degenerates into a heated exchange of opinion amounting to a quarrel, then you have come down the wrong road.
- As a leader you need to be able to generate and lead the kind of discussion that creates informed decisions. Remember, too, the great principle that the more that people share in making decisions that affect their working lives the more they are committed to carrying them out.
- Rational argument has long been studied by philosophers and you will benefit from their advice summarized in this chapter on how to avoid errors or fallacies in reasoning.
- You should be able to spot any deliberate attempts to mislead you by the use of 'tricks of the trade' – the sort of thing that unscrupulous politicians do.

The language of truth is simple.
German proverb

11

USEFUL ORIGINALITY

'To create is always to do something new.'
Martin Luther

New ideas are essential for industry, commerce and the public service. New products and new ways of doing things are the lifeblood of successful enterprise. The theme of this chapter is creative and innovative thinking, the means by which ideas are born and nurtured. Such ideas do not result from following clearly prescribed steps but they can be encouraged. In order to stimulate the synthesizing and holistic powers of mind you have to create the right conditions and apply certain principles.

WHAT IS CREATIVITY?

We all have new ideas. We vary, however, in terms of the *quantity* we produce in our lifetime, and still more in the *quality* of those ideas. People who have many new ideas with a high rate of excellent ones among them are called creative thinkers.

The word 'creative' should be bestowed rarely. It always implies a value judgement. Therefore we should separate in theory the two dimensions of creativity: quantity and quality. There are prolific novelists in most countries but we can all probably think of a writer who produced only a few works of real genius. Most creative thinkers can be placed on a scale in terms of a ratio of quality to quantity (see Creativity ratios, below).

An example of an A-type thinker is Dr R. Buckminster Fuller, the inventor, engineer, architect-designer and philosopher. After being expelled from Harvard and failing as a businessman he turned to architecture and invention. One of the most controversial architectural figures of our time, he produced designs for unprecedented types of structure that reflected his belief and optimism in the benefits of modern technology. Thus his Dymaxion House of 1927 saw the modern home not in terms of a walled structure but of technology servicing the human life within it. The house hung from a mast on a wire construction. The Dymaxion three-wheeled car of 1932 similarly rejected the traditional coach maker's craft to produce a futuristic design.

	High	A High productivity and few quality ideas	C Many quality ideas in high quality
PRODUCTIVITY OF IDEAS		B Not very productive and not producing many 'pearls'	D Many quality ideas with low productivity
	Low	QUALITY OF IDEAS	High

Creativity ratios

But none of Fuller's inventions caught on before he conceived the Geodesic Dome, a linking of triangles into a strong and lightweight sphere. It was another result of his relentless pursuit of architectural forms along the path of mathematical logic. Architects hailed it as a genuine advance and Fuller's public image as a lovable crackpot began to change. Unlike classic domes, Fuller's did not depend on heavy vaults or flying buttresses for support. The weight load was transmitted throughout the structure, producing a high strength-to-weight ratio. More than 2,000,000 domes have since been built.

What determines 'quality' in creative thinking? There are many definitions, but common to all is a social judgement of value, often in terms of the three great value families: goodness, truth and beauty. Here we are concerned primarily with the first – goodness. Useful originality is a branch of it. A good idea is one that a critical mass of people deem to be both useful and original.

There are two approaches to defining the creative person, which correspond to the inductive and deductive methods of reasoning. You can study many such individuals and try to generalize, or you can work downwards from the general principles and draw deductions from the general principles in this book. These are not alternatives; some combination of the two will yield the best results.

Either way it is a difficult exercise because creativity is not a discrete ability. It cannot be discovered by a process of analysis. It is a holistic combination of mental abilities and qualities of personality, temperament and character. At the heart of that combination, however, is synthesizing: the ability to combine together miscellaneous things into new wholes.

NECESSITY IS THE MOTHER OF INVENTION

We can learn a great deal from studying the qualities of creative thinkers. It is especially instructive to see how they scan their environment, deeply feeling its needs. New ideas are shaped, often using the depth mind principle, in response to a pressing need or an inconvenience.

Necessity certainly triggered off creative thinking in the mind of a butcher's clerk in Liverpool called Frank Hornby, who was born in 1863. He read Samuel Smiles' book *Self-Help* and took to making models for his children. The big breakthrough – combining self-help, engineering, models and children – came in 1900.

'One snowy Christmas Eve I was taking a long railway journey', wrote Hornby fifteen years later, 'and as I sat in my corner seat my mind was, as usual, turning over new schemes for my boys'enjoyment.' His immediate problem was a shortage of parts for a model crane he had begun to construct. And then, Eureka! Hornby had it! He would make the same kind of part, perforated with bolt-holes, so that it could be bolted in different positions and at different angles. 'I tell you, boys, that I was pleased when I hit upon this solution to our trouble, but I had no idea then that the few hours' close thought which I have given to my hobby were destined to change the entire future course of my life and work.'

Hornby called his invention Mechanics-Made-Easy and patented it in 1901. It was a simple idea – half-inch wide metal strips with bolt-holes half an inch apart – but immediately successful. In 1907 he coined the name Meccano. By the outbreak of the First World War Hornby had made a million and was earnestly outlining his philosophy in a small book entitled *Frank Hornby: the Boy who made a Million with a*

Toy. Samuel Smiles had not been forgotten: 'The Boy Scouts' idea is to do a helpful deed every day. Meccano is built on the principle of helpfulness. It gives every boy the opportunity to learn (while he is playing) how to do things that will help him to be successful when he becomes a man.' Indeed, the invention had many industrial applications; it was certainly more than a toy.

During the 1920s and 1930s Hornby's products invaded many European homes. Meccano sets grew larger and their models infinitely more complex. Meccano begat Hornby trains. Hornby trains begat Dinky toys. *Meccano* magazine, founded in 1916, grew to a circulation of 130,000 copies a month. There were editions in German and French; the Meccano Instruction Manual even ran to Russian and Cantonese.

The need to make educational toys for his own children was a sufficient spur or stimulus for Frank Hornby's depth mind to produce a creative synthesis of ideas and techniques. Sometimes an idea has to wait for a big enough need. The first zip fastener was demonstrated at the Chicago World's Fair of 1893, but had a number of defects, not least that it came apart easily. An improved version was tried out under the name C-Curity, but the zip did not catch on until the First World War, when the American armed services created a large market.

Many inventions come about as a response to a personal inconvenience. The carpet sweeper was put together in 1876 by Melville Bissell, a china-shop owner of Michigan, because he suffered from headaches brought on by the dusty straw used for packing his wares. The first ballpoint pen was devised in 1938 by a Hungarian journalist, Laszlo Biro, because he got bored with blotting his work.

Britain can lay claim to one invention that has revolutionized daily life. The world's first cannery was established in

1812 in Bermondsey, London. In those days canning was a job for expert craftsmen, the contents of the can being introduced through a hole in the top and sealed with a soldered disc. But there was one snag. The directions on the label read: 'Cut around the top near to the outer edge with a chisel and hammer . . .' There could be no better demonstration of the maxim 'Necessity is the mother of invention'. The tin-opener had to be invented.

Constantly taxed with being a genius, Thomas Edison gave some thought to the subject, coming up with the famous definition: 'Genius is one per cent inspiration and 99 per cent perspiration.' He enlarged on this to his secretary: 'Well, about ninety-nine per cent of it is a knowledge of the things that will not work. The other one per cent may be genius, but the only way that I know to accomplish anything is everlastingly to keep working with patient observation.'

Even with his phenomenal work rate, however, it is unlikely that most of us would come up with even one invention of the calibre of the light-bulb in the course of a lifetime. And he invented not only the light-bulb but the phonograph, the telephone (concurrently in competition with Bell), the means of distributing electrical power, X-ray plates, and so on and on until the very end of his life. The capacity of the man is almost unimaginable. He was able to conceive of machines for recording what we hear, which turned out to be the phonograph; for recording what we see, which became the movie camera, that were outside the realm of anything existing then, so that their conceptualization was a supreme work of imagination. Confronted with a problem, Edison was able to see how the solution might be arrived at. He could imagine, in the broadest terms, the short- and long-term consequences of his inventions. And all that lay between him and these goals was a great deal of hard work, which he could not wait to dispose of as soon as possible.

Edison's life was ruled by the excitement of the hunt. He once said to a colleague: 'Beach, I don't think Nature would be so unkind as to withhold the secret of a good storage battery if a real earnest hunt for it is made. I'm going to hunt.' And hunt he did, whether for the secret of the battery, the right filament for the incandescent bulb, the best mixture for insulating cables, or whatever the current problem might be, in the most methodical and exhaustive manner. There was never any time to spare; as soon as one problem was disposed of, another idea was waiting to be put to the test. There was never enough time – and he knew it – to investigate all his ideas. For example, in the end it was not Edison, but the Wright brothers, who made a successful aeroplane, although as early as 1889 Edison told a journalist:

> You can make up your mind . . . that these fellows who are fooling around with gasbags are wasting their time. The thing can't be done on those lines. You've got to have a machine heavier than air and then find something to lift it with. That's the trouble, though, to find the 'something'. I may find it one of these days.

WIDEN YOUR SPAN OF ANALOGY

The concept of width seems central to me. Our spans of analogy – the gap in time and space that our minds can bridge – vary considerably. Creative thinking often begins with the perception of a relationship – a spark of meaning – between two apparently unrelated things or ideas. 'The most original person is he who adapts from the most sources.'

I would amend that saying so that it reads '. . . from the widest apart sources'. Creative thinking, then, is bringing together things that are widely separated in time and/or space.

A classic illustration of the same principle at work is the invention of the seed drill by Jethro Tull, 'the greatest individual improver that British agriculture had ever known'. Tull was a musician and lawyer and went into farming out of necessity. Before his time sowing was done by means of a wheeled vehicle that held the seed in a container; and as the wheels turned the seed ran down through metal tubes or hollowed coulters underneath. The front of each coulter made a small furrow in the soil and the seed ran into it. A bush-harrow drawn behind the drill restored the soil and covered the seed. Earlier machines had failed because they could not effectively control the flow of seed from container to soil. Tull, the musician, solved the problem by adapting the mechanism on the sounding board of an organ to the drill he was making. He controlled the flow of the grain by means of a brass cover and adjustable spring, copied from the tongue in the organ mechanism.

The French doctor Laennec conceived and invented the stethoscope. The idea came to him when he remembered a boyhood incident of signalling to his friends by tapping out messages on a hollow log.

For the inventor a rich source of analogy is Nature itself. For Nature has creative and holistic properties embedded in its processes. Natural analogies can help you to discover or apply relevant principles. Try the following quiz:

Quiz: Inventions or developments

List specific inventions or developments that were (or might have been) suggested to creative thinkers by the following natural phenomena. (Turn to p. 181 for answers.)

(1) Human arms
(2) Cats
(3) Seagulls
(4) A frozen salmon
(5) Spiders
(6) Earthworms
(7) A flower
(8) The eye of a fly
(9) Conical shells
(10) Animal bone structures

Interest, observations, storage in memory and synthesis are therefore the key constituents of creative thinking. A wide span of analogy is essential.

THE DEPTH MIND DIMENSION

Synthesis of apparently unrelated things or ideas carried out at the conscious level is not the same as free-range, natural creative thinking. In the latter the process of synthesis takes place at a less than conscious level. The rudimentary idea itself may emerge from the depth mind, as it did in the case of Frank Hornby. Authors and poets report as much. C. Day Lewis once described the process in a lecture thus:

> What seems to happen for a poet is that experience sinks down on to the seabed of the unconscious. And lying there for a length of time, it is changed: 'those are pearls that were his eyes'. And one day a fragment of this buried treasure floats to the surface. It comes to me, very often, in an enigmatic form – a form of words, a brief phrase, which is attended by a special feeling of anticipation, excitement. It comes, more often than not, quite unexpectedly, when the mind is in neutral, or thinking of something else.

We have met a similar phenomenon, related to decision making, in the chapters on intuition and the depth mind.

You can see the same principle at work, but with much more emphasis on a holistic or growing synthesis – the conception of an idea followed by a period of gestation in the mind's womb.

The ability to put your mind into neutral is worth developing, for there is plenty of evidence to support the poet's contention that ideas come at unexpected, relaxed moments, when you are not pressurizing your mind for results.

Whenever the American businessman J. Pierpont Morgan had to make a decision and the key thought would not come to him, he would deliberately put the problem out of his mind by getting out a pack of cards and playing a solitaire game for an hour. During or after the game the right decision would occur to him. Morgan had developed a simple relaxation technique to unblock the powers of his depth mind.

Scores of people have made creative breakthroughs by programming their mind and letting the purposeful unconscious part of it work for them. When they have ceased straining for the answer it arrives in a flash, out of the blue, or as a hunch, while they are relaxing by doing something with hands or body. Agatha Christie claimed most of her ideas came to her while washing up. Many men have ideas while shaving. For other people they may come when driving or gardening. A British Nobel prize winner, Dr Godfrey Hounsfield, made the crucial breakthrough that led to the development of the body scanner while indulging in his favourite hobby, rambling. 'I'm very keen on rambling,' he said later. 'It's a time when things come to one, I find. The seeds of what happened came on a ramble.'

Edwin H. Land, the inventor of polaroid photography, also had his bright idea while walking:

I recall a sunny vacation day in Santa Fe, New Mexico, when my little daughter asked why she could not see at once the picture I had just taken of her. As I walked around that charming town I undertook the task of solving the puzzle she had set me. Within the hour, the camera, the film, and the physical chemistry became so clear to me that with a great sense of excitement I hurried over to the place where Donald Brown, our Patent Attorney (in Santa Fe by coincidence) was staying, to describe to him in great detail a dry camera which would give a picture immediately after exposure. In my mind it was nearly complete and so real that I spent several hours describing it, after which it was perhaps more real to him than even the ultimate reality.

Learning to relax and listen for the answer is a necessary condition for creative thinking. Times just before going to sleep or shortly after waking, when the body is in a state of complete relaxation, are often as fruitful as those of physical activity.

On rare occasions ideas come disguised as imagery during the course of a dream. Over a century ago Elias Howe alighted on the idea that led to the modern sewing machine. He worked on the machine for weeks, but one thing foiled him: how to thread the needle and still have the top of the needle attached to the machine. One night, after he had worked all day making no headway, he fell into an exhausted sleep. He began to dream that cannibals had captured him and ordered, 'You must perfect the sewing machine within twenty-four hours or be eaten.' The cannibals danced round him. Then he suddenly noticed that the spear held by the cannibal chief had a hole in the blade near the point. He woke up with a start. He had discovered the solution! Put the hole in the sewing machine needle at the bottom near the point instead of at the top as in the needles of his day.

New ideas, insights or hunches can spring from your

depth mind if you learn to interpose periods of hard mental work with times when you are lying fallow. Just lying down to sleep or relaxing in any other way without priming your unconscious with the question and data analysed as thoroughly as possible, will not produce anything worthwhile. We can apply here the principle of Louis Pasteur: 'Fortune favours the prepared mind'. But learning to unwind and to listen to your depth mind – trusting it in a warm and positive way to do its distinctive work – will take you forwards on your journey towards becoming a more creative person. Then, of course, when the creative idea has arrived you will be propelled into a great deal of hard work at the conscious level – possibly over years – to lick it into shape and bring the product or service to the market place.

IDEA BANKS

Having a special place to store ideas relating to a particular subject can be useful. This 'idea bank' can be a stiff covered book, a file, a shoe box, a desk drawer, or a combination of all these. Whenever you have a good idea, write it down and bank it. Then, when you get ready to start some serious 'imagineering' you will have several previous ideas to get you started.

For example, a single sentence copied into his notebook from one of his daughter's school-books gave author James Clavell the first bright idea for his novel *Shogun*. It said: 'In 1600 an Englishman named Will Adams came to Japan and became a samurai'. Clavell had been researching a book about modern-day Japan, but, intrigued by those words in the school text, he changed tack and immersed himself in learning about feudal Japan. Four years and 2,183 sheets of manuscript later Clavell had produced the 803-page best seller.

Use your ideas bank as a tool for creative reflection and thinking. Creativeness, as we have seen, implies bringing together things considered unrelated by conventional thought into an unprecedented dynamic relationship. The questioning, curious mind – innocent of intellectual subdivisions and conventional categorizings and taking everything interesting as grist to its mill – can cause us to bring diverse images, concepts and ideas together in a very fertile and stimulating way.

You will notice mysteriously creative constellations of elements on a couple of pages of your notebook, but the range of material they contain has the unlimited potential of a kaleidoscope of new combinations and associations. You can keep it all in a state of readiness by often browsing through them: ponder, dipping into them, glancing at a few pages last thing at night or on a train journey.

Going through your own jottings in this way is a much more intimate and profound process than dipping into other people's books, since the intuitive faculties have a much fuller part to play (and a more economical one, since everyone knows how maddeningly elusive ideas or facts are when you want them). Moreover, the original act of writing down the idea or morsel of information will help to commit it to your creative depth mind.

INNOVATION

The artist or inventor, the outstanding creative thinker in any field, differs from other people in degree, not in kind. As C. Day Lewis said:

The instinct to make something, to make something grow – a table, a baby, a gardening trellis or a scientific hypothesis – we know to be universal. However humble or exalted the thing made, however ephemeral or long-lived, it has come into being through the operation of the creative spirit. It is possible, and right, to take pride in something which is the work of many hands – a controlled experiment, a ship, an aircraft.

Most change is incremental rather than discontinuous. Innovation means not merely introducing novelties but making changes to something that is already established. An example of this more modest kind of creative change was the adding of milk to chocolate by Daniel Peter in 1867 to make milk chocolate. Innovation is an act that strives to produce small improvements on what is accepted today. It seeks newer and better solutions to old and current problems, solutions tied to a practical objective and geared to a measurable operational result. The development of the digital clock is a good example.

The need for innovation is universal. All products, whether goods or services, require constant renovation and improvement. For change is happening all around us, and it can suddenly outflank whole technologies. Think of the changes that the makers of timepieces and writing implements have had to cope with since the inventions of the pocketwatch and fountain pen. The insatiable appetite of the public for useful or 'added value' novelty helps to fuel that drive for innovation.

The universal need for innovation in industry and commerce, coupled with the fact that quite small changes can save costs or improve products, opens the door of creativity to all who care to enter.

The same principles apply in innovation as in creative thinking proper. Improvements may lie far afield in another country, another technology or even another time in history.

For example, there seems to be no connection between the method of supplying scattered American farmers in the mid-West pioneered in the 1920s by Sears, the US mail order giant, and the success today of Marks & Spencer, but that creative link exists. For Sears served as a model for Marks & Spencer, as described below.

In the 1920s, the American farmer had little time or opportunity to go shopping, and subscribed instead to a Sears catalogue giving the novel guarantee of 'your money back and no questions asked'. Offering this service also meant creating new human skills, for example by organizing suppliers to achieve new standards of efficiency. Sears further adapted itself in the 1920s to the vast new urban market by placing its stores on the outskirts of the cities. When Simon Marks visited America, and Sears, in 1924 he re-thought the objectives of his firm, which was to be nothing less than a social revolution: that is, providing upper-class goods of better-than-upper-class quality, but at prices the working and lower middle classes could afford.

Innovation requires a certain amount of humility. We have to build on others' contributions, and allow our own to be built on by others' contributions, and allow our own to be built on by others in turn. As the great physicist, Lord Rutherford, said, 'Every man depends on the work of his predecessors. When you hear of a sudden unexpected discovery – a bolt from the blue, as it were – you can always be sure that it has grown up by the influence of one man on another, and it is this mutual influence which makes the enormous possibility of scientific advance.'

Creativity is therefore a social activity. The creative person depends upon the work of predecessors and colleagues. A degree of unselfishness is necessary in all quality thinking.

MANAGEMENT ACTIONS

What can you do as a manager to encourage innovation around you? Here are some practical steps:

- Set an example by thinking about your own job and making some improvements. Remember, activity is not the same as action. Ships are not the only things that collect barnacles. Scrape them off your keel. If you change yourself, you will trigger off change about you.
- Look at your work team with a new eye. Sort out the innovators from those who have gone brown at the edges. Encourage each individual to come up with a quota of ideas.
- Work out a fair system for rewarding both the creative individual and the creative group. Small cash prizes may help. A few years ago, British Rail, for example, gave a £100 award to a train diver who suggested that the shiny metallic buttons on dustcoats issued to drivers for crawling around engines could be replaced by cheaper rubber composition ones. The idea saved about £2,000 a year.
- Set aside time now and then for meetings designed to think creatively about innovations. Submit to it a list of suggestions or problems offered by individuals for discussion. Take action on suggestions that seem promising.
- Develop an atmosphere of trust and warmth, a supportive and constructive climate where individuals are encouraged to think for themselves.

KEY POINTS: USEFUL ORIGINALITY

- New ideas are essential to all human enterprise. Creativity is about having new and valuable ideas; innovation is about bringing them to market in the form of improved or new products and services.
- Making analogies is often the trigger for new ideas. Creative thinking often begins with the perception of a relation – a spark of meaning – between two apparently unrelated things or ideas.
- Really creative people have a wide span of relevance: they look far afield, even to remote places or times in history, for solutions to their problems.
- It is important to think sideways, or laterally, because the seeds of a solution to a problem may lie outside the box you are working in.
- The sideways (or lateral) thinking involved often leads to reversing what appears to be the natural or logical way of doing things. For example, the earliest method of making cars involved teams of men moving from one car to another. Henry Ford turned it all upside down. He put the car frames on belts and moved them past the men – the birth of the assembly line.
- As a strategic leader, make sure you develop an ethos, climate or culture in your organization that breeds useful originality.

Mankind is pre-eminently creative, destined to strive consciously for a purpose and to engage in making – that is, incessantly and eternally to make new roads, wherever they may lead.

Dostoevsky

12

DEVELOPING YOUR THINKING SKILLS

'The development of general ability for independent
thinking and judgement should always be placed
foremost, not the acquisition of special knowledge.'
Albert Einstein

This chapter aims to inspire you to develop your thinking
skills. Doing this will contribute both to the success of your
career and also to your mental health and happiness. For
mental fitness is as important as physical fitness. Intellectual
activities, sports and games can help keep your mind in trim.

This book rests on the assumption that decision making
is fundamental to management. The actual decisions managers take vary enormously. If you analysed them many
would centre on the proper use of resources – people,
money, plant – to achieve the ends of the organization. What
those ends are at any given time, how you measure them,
and what your resources should be, are all matters meriting
hard managerial thought.

WHAT IS AN EFFECTIVE DECISION?

Before you can become a more effective decision maker you will need to reflect on the nature of an effective decision. It is not necessarily a perfect decision – if such a thing exists. But it should be the best decision you are capable of making in the circumstances. What do words such as *good*, *better* or *best* – value judgements all – mean in this context? They are evaluations based on the way the decision achieves the aim or objective you had in mind. Does the arrow hit the mark? Does the decision affect your purpose?

In many circumstances there is no one correct course of action: several paths lead to the top of the mountain. Here decision making contrasts sharply with mathematical problem solving; there is only one right answer to the problem 'What do 36 and 64 add up to?' Not so in management.

But that does not absolve the management of an organization from the hard intellectual effort of choosing a course that is best for them. For each organization is unique. Moreover, being effective in thinking rarely means copying successful competitors. It often entails going back to first principles, reflecting deeply on the changing situation and coming out with products that creatively blend the old with the new.

Ultimately, then, the test of a decision is whether or not it actually produces the goods. If it does, it is effective in the sense that it accomplishes the intention; it gives the desired result. The difficulty you may face as a manager is that by the time you are in a position to judge results it could be too late; you will have already made the wrong decision. Therefore you should know the characteristics that will make a decision *likely* to be effective before you make it. If you – or your organization – are deviating from these established norms during the process itself, then a red warning light should start flashing urgently in the cockpit of your individual – or the corporate – mind.

Because you cannot fully know the result of a decision before you take it you are exposed to a degree of uncertainty. You can foresee some consequences for certain, others with a degree of probability, and still others as possibilities. But there may be some that are hidden from you for one reason or other. You will have to live with them. Other contingencies may also be sprung on you. These can turn a good decision into a dead letter overnight. The actions of a competitor, a national strike and unforeseeable change in world prices: all these can intervene disastrously between a decision and its desired result. An effective decision maker will therefore take the unexpected into account. He or she will form a contingency plan that will enable them to modify their decision and to succeed in the face of the unexpected while still achieving the objective.

The risks involved, the sheer complexity of information and the balance of arguments for and against each course of action can breed indecision, the worst disease of corporate management. Prevention is better than cure. It may help you to remain decisive if you remember that in the nature of things managers must decide and decide quickly if so required.

Business is sometimes like a battlefield in that there is often no obviously right decision, just competing alternatives and a pressure to decide. It is better to make a wrong decision if it gets things moving than to make no decision at all. You can steer a moving ship. The alternative is inertia. If a wrong decision is made it can often be corrected as soon as the mistake becomes apparent. That is the principle of trial-and-error, an invaluable strategy for those who do not know what to do next.

The fear of getting it wrong creates a climate in which anxiety, delay and indecision take root. Paradoxically, many books and courses on rational decision making, often replete with algebraic equations, can feed that fear of getting it wrong. You need confidence to make decisions. That means ridding yourself of the fear of making mistakes. Of course you will make mistakes but that is better than doing nothing.

No manager in their right senses actually intends to make mistakes. All will benefit from a checklist to ensure that they remain in the flightpath of the effective decision. Here are some key questions for your own checklist:

- Have I defined the objective?
- Do I have sufficient information?
- What are the feasible options?
- Have I evaluated them correctly?
- Does this decision feel right now I have begun to implement it?

When you do make a mistake, turn your regrets into gold. Go back to your checklist and try to identify precisely where you went wrong. Then you will be learning by experience. That in turn will programme your depth mind. The next time that red light will flash sooner.

THE GOAL OF CONSENSUS

Leadership is not solely about getting the intellectual quality of a decision right, important though this may be. It is about getting results through people. Therefore the leader will need to include other people in the process of decision making. For a decision will be effective only if it is fully implemented. People are more likely to put their hearts into it if they have shared either explicitly or implicitly in the making of that decision.

People can participate in the early stages of the process, leaving the leader to take the final decision. They can, for example, contribute information or suggest a possible solution. How far a leader should go in sharing a decision with another person or a group depends on certain key factors: the kind of decision it is, the knowledge and experience of those concerned, and situational factors such as the time available for consultation.

Taking these factors into account there will be circumstances, especially as you rise up the promotion ladder, when you will want consensus. Yet many managers are not clear what consensus means in this context. Here is a definition:

When the feasible courses of action have been debated thoroughly by the group and everyone is prepared to accept that in the circumstances one particular solution is the best way forward, even though it might not be *every* person's preferred solution.

The most important test is that everyone is prepared to *act* as though it was their preferred course of action.

Granted a common commitment among group members to the purpose and aims of the organization – a shared set of values – and an absence of aggressive or arrogant egoism in individual group members, consensus is usually forthcoming if a leader seeks it with determination and skill.

WHAT IS AN EFFECTIVE THINKER?

Proper decision making by individuals, groups and organizations presupposes a high level of basic thinking skills. Let's recall the main elements of productive thinking. The skills of *analysing* are constantly at work, breaking down larger entities into their component parts, sifting information and abstracting from it conclusions. When you are developing courses of action you are *synthesizing*, putting things together. When you are seeking new ideas of combinations it is best to restrain deliberately from being critical – to suspend judgement. For ideas, like newborn lambs need a warm and encouraging climate. At the constructive core of criticism and all other forms of judgement lies *valuing*, the assessing of relative worth. Lastly, the mind operates on different levels. A holistic approach – aided by a period of unconscious gestation – may help to produce the right decision for you: the pattern will grow in your mind and break surface in clarity.

An effective thinker should know which kind of thinking is needed at a given time and be able to do it themselves or participate in it. For example, if you want to think up a name for a new product it may be best to brainstorm it. Other types of problem may require very sophisticated forms of analysis.

The effective thinker knows that decisiveness does not always mean quick decisions. He or she is committed to think it through. The success or failure of some industries often depends on a small number of key decisions – perhaps only one or two a year – and if these are wrong or not as good as they might have been, no number of subsidiary decisions can fully correct the situation. These key decisions – such as whether to join forces with a foreign competitor or to take a major innovative step to match competition – are vital from the strategic viewpoint. They must be studied with a scientific objectivity, employing all the methods of analysis and projection used in a fully professional manner. The options and the data, the arguments for and against each option, should be debated in conceptual forums among managers at senior level long before the issue comes to the boardroom for decision. This cannot be done properly if senior management spend nearly all their time dealing with day-to-day problems of a short-term nature. If they delegate properly they will have time for proper strategic thinking.

Decision making, in the shorter or longer term, does not exhaust the role of thinking in management. There remains problem solving in the narrow sense of sorting out systems-type problems, such as those posed by technology. There is the much wider contribution of the intuitive and imaginative powers, the opportunity-seeking and opportunity-creating faculties. Without them the progress of your enterprise will grind to a halt. Do you encourage them enough?

No one person has all these intellectual gifts. By accident or design, however, they will be present in a really high quality top management team. We must all learn the social skills that allow us to combine forces effectively with thinkers of complementary talent in the same organization or outside it. Thinking is teamwork.

What then is an effective thinker? He or she is skilled in analysing, synthesizing and valuing; knows when and how to use their depth mind; and is receptive to intuition. Effective thinkers' imaginations can be brought into play to find new ways forward in apparently baffling situations. On occasion, creative solutions will come to them mainly as a result of careful preliminary work. They are open to new ideas, even those suggested by unlikely analogies: their span of relevance is wide. Lastly, they are humble enough to know that others will surpass them in some thinking skills and in specialized knowledge, and so they are able to link their minds with others in the search for truth.

MAKING AN INVENTORY OF YOUR SKILLS

Improvement is always a relative notion. At any given time a person starts from a certain baseline. Their mental faculties are genetic endowments; education will have drawn them out and trained them. The relative importance of these two aspects – nature and nurture – in a person's mental history is much debated. Opinions change as researchers produce their findings. What is clear, however, is that both are significant. Natural aptitude has to be there, especially for the more specialized forms of thinking such as music or mathematics. But education of quality is essential for the general development of each individual's mind.

The first principle of self-development is 'know thyself'. Establish your baseline. You know yourself better than anyone else. What is your record of achievement as a thinker? What did your school reports, other feedback from staff and examination performance, tell you about your interests, aptitudes and temperament? Since leaving school or university in what ways have you grown in one or more of the three related fields of applied thinking: decision making, problem solving and creative thinking? Again, what does the feedback of colleagues – formal or informal – tell you about your areas for improvement? I suggest you write this information down on one side of a sheet of paper now, being as specific as you can.

Now turn the sheet over and list what you consider to be your good and your bad habits as a thinker. For bad mental habits – such as slipshod reasoning, making false assumptions, jumping to conclusions or not listening properly – can be unconsciously picked up all too easily. Check this list with a colleague at work and with your spouse or best friend.

LEARNING ON THE JOB

How do you acquire good habits? In the same way you received your bad ones – from observing others. You may not work closely with outstanding practical thinkers but you can still learn a great deal from observing and reflecting on the living case studies around you: the senior managers to whom you are responsible, your colleagues and your team members. Don't ignore the latter: they may have had the benefit of more education and professional training than you. Why not profit from it?

Good thinking habits revolve like planets around the sun of truth. As a manager you can do no better than to emulate Lord Thomson, of whom a senior colleague wrote: 'his most memorable quality was his instinctive habit of telling the truth. His strength, which was very great, particularly in dark moments, made him enjoy truth when another man would have found illusion more comfortable. He always faced reality and he always believed that he could do good business in terms of the reality that he faced.'

These associated habits of seeking and speaking the truth have one incalculable benefit in human relations, one that far outweighs all the mental effort required to see reality, and the moral courage sometimes needed if you are going to respond to it with the appropriate action. Truth begets trust. Trust is the bedrock of partnership.

In order to learn about what, for example, original thinking or imaginative thinking or effective decision making means at work, we rely upon experience. You cannot learn those things at school from schoolmasters or at university from academics. Managers are your teachers, if only by example. It may be your good fortune to work closely with a business person of genius – provided you observe them closely.

Alfred Sloan worked with William C. Durant, the founder of General Motors. He recalled that Durant 'would proceed on a course of action guided solely, as far as I could tell, by some intuitive flash of brilliance. He never felt obliged to make an engineering hunt for facts'. Sloan, perhaps the greatest manager of his day, concluded: 'The final act of business judgement is intuitive.'

May I emphasize here the recommendation made in the last chapter for keeping a notebook in which to enter your tentative conclusions, helpful examples, principles, new ideas, management proverbs and so on. Make notes from the books or articles you read that have a bearing upon the subject. Try to imagine what mental habits you would like to have developed at the end of three years: list them in your book. Go through your notebook carefully every month or so, looking backwards to see what else you have learnt. Think about thinking – it is your profession.

KEEP MENTALLY FIT

Profession, work, occupation – these dominate our lives. But the day will come when you will stop managing. Without the mental stimulus of decision making at work, will your brain continue to be healthy? Most of our brains don't get enough exercise. They are like muscles that need to be used and stretched if they are to remain healthy. Exercises of a mental kind, if done regularly, will help to keep your mind in trim.

We lose some of our brain cells every day. People whose

jobs require cerebral thinking such as lawyers, professors and doctors, lose fewer cells daily than people in other professions.

The best way to maintain good blood circulation in your head, which prevents cell loss, is through using your brain. Thinking is an essential therapy. We all need to develop mental equivalents to daily physical exercise such as walking briskly or jogging. Mental exercise, like physical exercise, should be as interesting and as much fun as possible: that way you are likely to persevere longer with it. Start with reading some demanding non-fiction books. Make notes; argue with the author; draw your own conclusions.

HOW TO AVOID STIMULUS DEFICIENCY

Few – perhaps none – of us are entirely self-motivating as thinkers. We need the outside stimulus that comes from other minds. Besides providing you with the stimulus to think for yourself other people can also give you new ideas. Again it is worth quoting Lord Thomson, for he capitalized on this fact, as every sensible manager should:

> I try to make friends wherever I go and it is my fond belief that I usually succeed. The way I look at it, everyone has an idea and one in a dozen may be a good idea. If you have to talk to a dozen people to get one good idea, even just the glimmering of an idea, that isn't wasteful work. People are continually passing things on to me, because I have given them to believe that I will be interested, I might even pay for it! Sometimes, usually when it is least expected, something comes up that is touched with gold.

Seek new experiences. Ruts and routines are the enemies of mental fitness: they induce staleness and rigidity. These will turn eventually into mental arthritis if you do nothing. A fresh challenge can bring life flooding back into the dry cells of your mental battery.

New experience is especially vital for the manager who has been in the same job for more than five years. Sometimes the job or its context changes so markedly that interest is renewed; sometimes it remains static and becomes boring. Sustained boredom, needless to say, is a killer of brain cells. Ask for promotion or a sideways move or to be sent on a course – anything to restore your freshness of vision, enthusiasm and appetite for work. If your requests are ignored, explore the option of changing your job. There could be risks involved in pursuing that course of action. But there are also risks in allowing yourself to vegetate gently in a job that no longer provides you with any intellectual challenge. Avoid terminal mental lethargy.

SUMMARY

How far you develop your abilities as a practical and productive thinker is largely up to you. Your starting point in terms of natural mental aptitudes and academic record is not as important now as your motivation to succeed as a manager.

If it has done nothing else I hope this book will have made you think – and think hard – about the core function of your trade as a manager: effective decision making. Above all, it should have made you want to exert yourself as a practical thinker.

You should deliberately stretch yourself to learn all you can about the art of making decisions. Even if you don't have many original ideas yourself, you should at least set yourself the goal of understanding more fully the creative process and how ordinary people can contribute to it. The future of industry, indeed the future of our civilization, depends upon the creative flair and innovative genius of people.

Decision making has to be learnt on the job, partly from wise practitioners in the craft and partly by personal experience. As experience accumulates you will be able to move with greater sureness and speed, although – as in all worthwhile fields of human life – there is always more to be learnt. We can always widen our interests, both for profit and pleasure. Work should be the chief outlet for your educated talents. But a sensible self-development programme, based on a realistic estimate of your abilities, interests and temperament, will both enhance your contribution at work and enrich your whole life beyond it.

KEY POINTS: DEVELOPING YOUR THINKING SKILLS

- 'I love thinking', wrote the science fiction writer Isaac Asimov, 'and writing is just thinking through your fingers'. I hope that this book has made you fall in love with clear thinking and has made you want to develop your thinking skills.
- By this point in our journey together you should have a good idea of your strengths and weaknesses – areas for improvement – as a thinker. As always, the principle is to build on your strengths and starve your weaknesses.
- You will get nowhere in your self-development without feedback. This will come from two sources: life and other people. The former will take the form of the consequences – both expected and unexpected – of the decisions you make. Reflect on these experiences in the light of the principles in this book, and learn your lessons.

- Take a piece of paper and write down the feedback you have received from others about you as a thinker – I mean an applied thinker and decision maker. Is there a pattern in the comments you have received? What are your tendencies?
- Who are the people who – by their example or their teachings – can help you to become more effective in this, the mental branch of leadership? Remember, tall experienced leaders have something to teach you if you have a listening ear.
- Humility is the quality that keeps you always open to learn more. It is the necessary condition for excellence in leadership.

In conclusion, therefore, you know your intellectual strengths and weaknesses. Now use that self-knowledge to develop the foundation on which to build your mind, using the principles set out in this book. Reread it at least twice. Don't expect too much and don't attempt too little. And for encouragement when the going is hard, remember the old proverb: 'God is with those who persevere'.

Learning is its own exceeding great reward.
William Hazlitt

ANSWERS

EXERCISE 1: Who Is Going to Barker Street? p. 15

The baker is Bob Barker. Bert's last name is Burke. Bart Burger is going to Barker Street.

Taxi Number	First Name	Last name	Profession	Wife's name	Destination
1	Brad	Bunger	barber	Betty	Baker St
2	Bob	**Barker**	baker	Beatrice	Burton St
3	Bart	Burger	banker	Barbara	**Barker St**
4	Brian	Baker	butcher	Brenda	Burbon St
5	Bert	Burke	broker	Bernice	Barton St

From clues 2, 4, 6, 7 and 11, we know: Barbara's husband gets into the third taxi, the last taxi goes to Barton Street, the butcher gets into the fourth taxi, Bob gets into the second taxi, and Mr Bunger gets into the first taxi. The remainder of the puzzle can be solved only by combining clues and eliminating possibilities.

You know that the butcher is in the fourth taxi, so Mr Burger (Clue 16) must be in the third taxi. And since Mr Burger gets into the third taxi, Brenda must be the wife of the man in the fourth taxi (Clue 10).

The next step is to combine clues 5 and 9. Burton Street is the home of Beatrice Barker; therefore, the only place these clues will fit is under taxi number two.

Clue 12 is next. Mr Baker must get into the fourth taxi since it is the only place where a last name and destination are still not found.

Clue 14, logically, follows. Since the barber lives in Baker Street (Clue 13), and is three taxis in front of Brian (Clue 15), the only place the barber could be is in the first taxi. Therefore, Brian's last name is Baker.

Since Bernice is married to the broker (Clue 8), the only place for these two items of information, by elimination, is under taxi number five.

By elimination, taxi number three now accommodates Clue 3 (Bart is the banker).

The only place Clue 1 now fits is taxi number one.

WHAT IT TAKES FOR TOP JOBS p. 27

Ranking of most valuable attributes at the top level of management	Attribute developed mainly by academic work	Attribute developed mainly by professional experience
1 Ability to take decisions	1	9
2 Leadership	0	9
3 Integrity	1	6
4 Enthusiasm	1	6
5 Imagination	1	6

Ranking of most valuable attributes at the top level of management	Attribute developed mainly by academic work	Attribute developed mainly by professional experience
6 Willingness to work hard	3	3
7 Analytical ability	7	2
8 Understanding of others	0	9
9 Ability to spot opportunities	1	8
10 Ability to meet unpleasant situations	0	9
11 Ability to adapt quickly to change	1	9
12 Willingness to take risks	0	8
13 Enterprise	1	4
14 Capacity to speak lucidly	4	5
15 Astuteness	1	9
16 Ability to administer efficiently	1	9
17 Open-mindedness	2	6
18 Ability to 'stick it'	3	4
19 Willingness to work long hours	3	3
20 Ambition	2	5
21 Single-mindedness	3	5
22 Capacity for lucid writing	9	1
23 Curiosity	4	3
24 Skill with numbers	7	2
25 Capacity for abstract thought	7	2

EXERCISES 2–6: How good is you logical thinking? p. 38

2. Either the first or the fourth statements must be true, because they cannot both be untrue. Therefore either Mr Carpenter or Mr Mason is the painter.

Since the second and third statements must both be untrue, Mr Mason is the carpenter, Mr Carpenter the painter and Mr Painter the mason.

3. Each barber must have cut the other's hair. The logician picked the barber who had given his rival the better haircut.

4. The parrot was deaf.

5. Among the 97 per cent of the women, if half wear two earrings and half none, this is the same as if each wore one. Assuming that each of the 800 women is wearing one earring, there are 800 earrings.

6. The trains are travelling one at 60 mph and one at 40 mph towards each other. Between them they will cover 100 miles in one hour. Therefore they will meet after one hour. The plane is flying backwards and forwards at 80 mph for one hour. Therefore the plane is flying at 80 mph for one hour. With this reorganization of relationships within the problem you should be able to work out the answer for yourself.

Think it through 1 p. 40

1. Carry cat to car and return empty-handed.
2. Carry Sara to car and return with cat.
3. Leave cat in house and carry Roger to car.
4. Return empty-handed and carry cat to car.

Think it through 2 p. 42

(a) How old is the Naval Captain? – 52
(b) What is the nationality of the football player? – Dutch

Profession	Nationalities	Ages	Sports	Destinations
Engineer	Dutch	40	Football	Birmingham
Teacher	Italian	24	Swimming	Manchester
Journalist	English	32	Volleyball	London
Singer	German	21	Athlete	Newcastle
Captain	French	52	Handball	Plymouth

This is one way of solving the problem:

Keep working through the facts from 1–14 in sequence.
Concentrate on clues for which there is only one answer.
That is:

1 The Engineer is seated on the extreme left.
2 The volleyball player is seated in the middle.
14 The Engineer is seated next to the Italian.

Then look for information that has only two possible answers. That is:

11 The passenger from France is seated next to the German.

If you place the Frenchman in the middle and the German on his right you are wrong. You can progress but will not be able to complete the whole problem.

If you place the German on the far right and the Frenchman next to him you are correct and you can progress logically, since you will find that other items of information now have only one answer. That is:

3 The Englishman is the journalist.
7 The handball player is French.

8 The passenger from Holland is bound for Birmingham.

13 The 24-year-old passenger is seated next to the passenger who is travelling to Birmingham.

Then look for other information which has only two possible answers. That is:

5 The teacher's sport is swimming.

If you place the teacher next to the engineer you are correct and can progress logically. If you place the teacher on the far right you are wrong and will be unable to solve the problem. It will be necessary to return to this point and take the other alternative.

If you have placed the teacher next to the engineer then progress logically to find other items of information that have only one answer.

10 The athlete is bound for Newcastle.

There is now a blank space in sports, so from the information at the beginning of the problem:

The man from Holland must play football.

6 The naval captain is travelling to Plymouth.

4 The singer is 21.

9 The passenger bound for London is 32.

12 The 40-year-old passenger is seated next to the passenger who is bound for Manchester.

The Captain is therefore 52.

EXERCISE 7: The missing space rocket p. 44

My suggested solution:

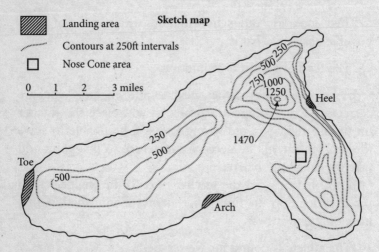

I would commit my team to a landing in the west at Toe, taking the good southerly route overland to the search area to reach it, according to calculations on the figures provided in the test, at around 17.30 hours, well over an hour before the enemy submarine is expected even to reach the island (at sunset, 18.45 hours).

(The test says the boats could be rowed at only up to 2 mph. The easier southerly overland route could be crossed at 4 mph but the other possible routes at only 3 mph. The cliffs in the north east could be climbed at about 90 metres per hour.)

My course of action would avoid the risk in an ill-equipped climbing party scaling the cliffs at Heel and the delays and exhaustion in rowing 10 kilometres from the cargo boat in rough seas to Arch, the southerly landing point.

I dismissed alternative plans which involved dividing my team and trying to deal with the opposition for one reason. The submarine was aware it had been spotted, so there was little prospect of surprising the landing party. There was no certainty which landing point the submarine would choose.

EXERCISE 8: An option problem p. 112

The flight engineer decided to work through the standard checklist yet again. Engines restarted when the aircraft was at 800 ft.

Quiz: Inventions or developments p. 150

1. A young English designer named Carwardine approached the firm of Herbert Terry at the beginning of the 1930s with the proposal that they should build a desk light employing the constant-tension jointing principles found in the human arm. The company agreed, and the Anglepoise light was the result. From that time it has been in production, scarcely altered except for details and finishes.

2. Cat's eyes in the road.

3. Spitfires.

4. Clarence Birdseye took a vacation in Canada and saw some salmon that had been naturally frozen in ice and then thawed. When they were cooked he noticed how fresh they tasted. He borrowed the idea and the mighty frozen food industry was born.

5. They could have suggested the principle of independent suspension.

6. The burrowing movement of earthworms has suggested

a new method of mining, which is now in commercial production.

7. In the Royal Botanic Garden Edinburgh there is a plaque commemorating a flower that inspired the design of the Crystal Palace.

8. Sir Basil Spence, the architect of Coventry Cathedral, was flipping through the pages of a natural history magazine when he came across an enlargement of the eye of a fly, and that gave him the general lines for the vault.

9. Linear motors.

10. Ball-and-socket joints.

ACKNOWLEDGEMENTS

The following publishers were kind enough to give permission for the reproduction of copyright material:

Hamish Hamilton Ltd: the extracts from *After I was Sixty* by Lord Thomson (Hamish Hamilton, 1975) used in Chapters 4, 9, 11 and 12.

INDEX

Visit **www.panmacmillan.com** to read more about all our books and to buy them. You will also find features, author interviews and news of any author events, and you can sign up for e-newsletters so that you're always first to hear about our new releases.